BASIC SOURCES
FOR
FAMILY HISTORY

1: BACK TO THE EARLY 1800s

Andrew Todd

First published April 1987

Reprinted with minor amendments July 1987

2nd edition March 1989

3rd edition May 1994

ALLEN & TODD, 9-11, Square Street, Ramsbottom, Bury, Lancashire BL0 9BE

'They who derive their worth from their ancestors resemble potatoes, the most valuable parts of which are underground.'

[Remark made by Lord Bacon, rediscovered by the Todmorden historian John Travis.]

To both Isabellas, great grandmother and daughter.

Researching into my own family's modest origins has taught me more real history than over 25 years spent both as victim and perpetrator of history teaching.

Cover drawing by AAT

CONTENTS

ISBN 0 948781 10 6

ACKNOWLEDGMENTS

The designs of the birth, marriage and death certificates illustrated on pages 62-3 and 64-5 are Crown-copyright and are reproduced with the permission of the Controller of Her Majesty's Stationery Office.

The census returns on pages 30-1 and 32 and are Crown-copyright material in the Public Record Office (HO107/2226 and HO107/1032) and are reproduced by permission of the Controller of Her Majesty's Stationery Office.

I am grateful for the many offers of encouragement to get on with 'the next one!'

BOOK REFERENCES AND ADDRESSES

Gibson (1) - Full book references are given at the end of each chapter.

(*) - An asterisk in the text refers to the addresses section on pages 92-3.

1 HOW FAR BACK CAN YOU GO?

The statistics of ancestry are staggering. Behind every living human being, there stands an army of vanished ancestors. Few people have personal knowledge of this vast host beyond their own grandparents. Even young children understand why they have four grandparents - two for each parent. Yet most people can go through life without following the mathematics of ancestry through to the logical conclusion.

On average, three generations fill a century (ie a person is about 100 years old when his or her great grandchildren are born). So a man born in 1966 will have parents born around 1933, four grandparents born about 1900, and eight great grandparents born around 1866.

This doubling up of ancestors at each generation stretches our imagination. There is an old puzzle which asks that if you put a grain of wheat on the first square of a chess board, two on the second, four on the third, eight on the fourth ... and so on ... how many grains must you put on the 64th? The answer is something like 'more grains than there are atoms in the universe'.

If 25 generations of people have lived since the year 1100, then you must have had around 33 million direct ancestors alive at that time. Since the population of England and Wales at the time of the Domesday Survey (1085-6) is estimated at 1.25 million, there is clearly a major problem. If we count back a further 25 generations, to the time of Roman Britain and then another 50 to the construction of Stonehenge, we have comfortably exceeded the contemporary population of the world at the time - human, animal and possibly even insect.

Intermarriage of cousins explains this apparent mathematical impossibility: a child of first cousins has one (and usually two) great grandparents who figure in both his mother's and father's family trees. So each union of first cousins usually duplicates 25% of their children's ancestry.

The problem, and its solution, is neatly illustrated by the arrival, in 1790, of a handful of British sailors and their Tahitian mistresses on the uninhabited Pitcairn Island, after the *Bounty* mutiny. Their descendants, after six generations of isolation, could claim 64 *Bounty* ancestors on their pedigrees; and the seventh generation will have 128, even though the number of 1790 arrivals must remain a constant.

We are all descended from a fairly small number of people. Hundreds of millions of us have some English or Welsh ancestry and are therefore descended from that 1.25 million alive in 1085/6. It was calculated that Edward III (reigned 1327-1377) had about 100,000 living descendants in 1900 (hence his title of 'the Clapham Junction' of Genealogy, since so many family trees connect up to him.) Edward I (1277-1307) was put down for one million by 1900. (Ironically, however, the much married Henry VIII (1509-1547) has no living descendants - unless there was illegitimate issue unknown to historians, and this is unlikely since kings tended to acknowledge their bastards.)

So we all belong to very large families. We must be distantly related to almost everyone we pass in the street.

If you reveal that you are tracing your family tree, you will always be asked how far back you have got. There are two answers to this, depending on what you are tracing:

1) **The direct male line** (ie your father's father's father and so on - the extreme left hand file on this book's cover). Most people start with an overriding interest in this - it is normally the source of your surname. In nine cases out of ten, you should manage to trace a line back to a couple who were born before 1830, at a time when the fastest method of travel was by horse. Some people have pushed one or more of their lines, with certainty, back to the reign of Henry VIII, and even earlier. A few less fortunates have difficulty in penetrating the 1800s.

2) **All your ancestral lines.** Despite medieval European laws of inheritance which emphasised direct male ancestry, each line contributes equally to your genetic make up. Each line will be different. No matter where you or your parents were born, you will find that your more remote ancestors will have originated from many different areas. I was born of Manchester parents and all four of my grandparents were Mancunians - yet their known ancestors came from towns and villages throughout Lancashire, and beyond - Cheshire, Yorkshire, Durham, Northumberland, Nottinghamshire, Derbyshire, Leicestershire, Warwickshire, Suffolk, Cambridgeshire, Wales and Ireland. Each line is represented by a fresh surname. Some prove easier to follow than others. This is a good reason to tackle all of them - when you reach a full stop on one, switch to another, gain experience, and come back to the problems when you know more.

Why are some families easier to trace than others? There are four main factors:

1) **APPEARANCE IN RECORDS** - if your great grandson were tracing his ancestors in 100 years time, he would have to rely on records which are now being compiled.

You will be an easy person to trace if you

    a) own a car, license and insure it, change it regularly, and always report changes of ownership to the DVLC at Swansea.

    b) have a steady job with a large employer.

    c) have lived in one house for many years, are on the electoral register, and pay the Council Tax.

    d) have a telephone.

    e) intend to leave a will, which will name a number of your relatives.

    f) are married and have legitimate children whose births are legally registered.

    g) are interested in your own ancestry, and intend to leave a copy of your family tree to your children and grandchildren. (By the time you have read this book, you will have decided that this is a satisfying and fairly straight-forward proposition.)

You will **not** be an easy person to trace if you

    a) do not own a car, or own one which is unlicensed, uninsured, and unknown to the DVLC.

    b) move from one job to another in the black economy.

    c) live in rented flats, rarely stay in one for more than a year or two, have never bothered about registering to vote, and intend studiously to avoid paying the Council Tax.

d) don't own a telephone.

e) don't intend to leave a will.

f) are not legally married, and have children who are not legally registered.

g) don't care about your family's history, throw away old photographs, letters and documents, and discourage your children from asking you what you can remember about your grandparents.

It follows that your ancestors will be easier to trace if they regularly appear in records kept when they were alive. You will be amazed at the wealth of records that have been kept, have survived, and are now open to public inspection. Britain has had no major political upheaval since the Civil War in the mid-17th Century, so (with certain exceptions) can boast one of the finest sets of public and county records in the world. Some people assume that their family's past is lost because no family documents survive. Official records, however, contain references to everybody's ancestors. I have a photocopy of the will of my earliest known ancestor - William LADIMAN, a Suffolk maltster born in the Tudor period. (The West Suffolk Record Office charged me about 20p for it.) My great grandfather, this man's direct descendant, was the last of my ancestors to be born in Suffolk. When he died in Manchester in 1926, he left not a jot of documentary information about his forbears (he was illiterate) - not even the name of his father. The past had to be reconstructed almost solely from official records.

If your ancestors stayed in one area, kept to one occupation, had their children registered by a moderately literate parish clerk, left the occasional will, owned some property, and sometimes had a gravestone erected to mark their parents' grave, then you too may get back to the reigns of the Tudors.

This discussion of records may have left you with the impression that solid, respectable, and wealthy ancestors are the easiest to trace. In fact, the humblest classes are very well documented - claimants of parish relief, criminals (who were found out), lunatics and common soldiers (always a lowly profession in this country prior to the 20th Century) appear in some very informative records.

The next factor, however, cuts across all the social classes:

2) SURNAMES - an unusual surname is a great asset. I've successfully followed families with rare names like BEADSMOORE, LANGSTROTH and LADIMAN back 300 years or more. Names deriving from small villages may be especially helpful to their genealogically-minded bearers.

Surnames ending in *-by*, *-ham*, *-ley*, *-shaw*, *-thorpe*, *-ton* and *-worth* are the most common of those which come from place names in England. Bartholomew's *Gazetteer of the British Isles* (available in most libraries) lists place names down to the smallest cluster of houses and can pinpoint the origin of such surnames - this provides a long term target of establishing ancestry in the district where that place lies.

Even common surnames may not pose too many problems if the family has stayed in one area or has been associated with a particular trade. I know a retired sea captain and deputy harbour master at Scarborough, called SMITH, who can easily push his ancestry back to a family of 18th Century shipbuilders in that port.

Surnames fanned out from their area of medieval origin. A nationally rare name like DAKIN was so common in the group of parishes in Derbyshire from which it sprang that problems of identification arise: it will be difficult to distinguish one John DAKIN from another before the detailed records of the 19th Century appear.

3) **MOBILITY** - pre-19th Century migration can be difficult to trace. Fortunately, most of it was over a short distance, between adjacent or nearly adjacent parishes. Long distance movement is the greatest hindrance to successful research, so it is as well that most big moves occurred in the railway age by which time national censuses were compiled in sufficient detail to allow the birthplace of each individual to be pinpointed.

The commonness of migration in the 75 years before the Great War is one of the delights, as well as the bugbear, of family history research - you are sure to be introduced to unfamiliar and unanticipated towns, but particularly villages. The 1911 census of England and Wales revealed that over a third of men had left their native county; and few of the 150 counties and county boroughs had not been connected by a move.

4) **OCCUPATIONS** - occupational mobility is also important. Where sons followed fathers, research is immeasurably easier. The name LOW is very common in South Lancashire, but I found that my LOWs in Bury were coalminers to a man - Robert was a collier in the 1700s, and a hundred years later so were many of his great grandsons. This helped me to piece together a very extensive tree of his descendants. Jobs involving specific skills and equipment were also generally hereditary. My wife's ancestors were Yorkshire coast fishermen and their direct descendants are still fishing from Scarborough, Filey and Flamborough, maintaining a tradition of at least three centuries.

Where families stayed put like this, you have to be prepared for the discovery of staggeringly large family trees. Look back at this book's cover and invert it in your own mind. A man alive in 1700 with two children should have ...

4 grandchildren by 1733

8 great grandchildren by 1766

16 great great grandchildren by 1800

32 great great great grandchildren by 1833

64 great great great great grandchildren by 1866

128 great great great great great grandchildren by 1900

256 great great great great great great grandchildren by 1933

512 great great great great great great great grandchildren by 1966.

So, by the present day, some 1,000 distant cousins will be able to claim descent from this one 1700 progenitor. This is a very conservative estimate - you will soon find that before the widespread use of contraception this century, families were much bigger. Eight children were as common as 2.2 are today and most survived, after the mid-19th Century, to have families of their own.

Some researchers become fascinated by these sorts of calculations: they abandon the idea of pushing their lines back in time and instead try to bring their trees forward, looking for all descendants of an ancestral couple. A Darwen student of mine found that his great great grandfather was a 19th Century Polish immigrant with the unlikely name of DUMKOPF. Finding a dozen or so of this name throughout the whole country in the modern telephone directories, he had to satisfy his curiosity and contact them. He established that they were all descendants of this one Polish immigrant, yet now scattered throughout Britain.

A friend of mine has been slotting MOIZERs onto a huge roll of wallpaper for years. He reckons they all descend from one 17th Century couple, and takes delight in ringing MOIZERs up all over the country to explain to them how they fit.

Contacts like this between long sundered branches of a family can produce spectacular results. My wife Irene's direct ancestor, Thomas GIBBONS, died of Influenza in Manchester in 1842, leaving not the slightest hint of where he had come from. This first industrial city attracted migrants from all over the country - so that ancestral line was at a dead end. Then contact with one Trevor GIBBONS through a family history society revealed the existence of the family bible of a GIBBONS family of Rowsley in Derbyshire - and this indicated that our Thomas was a younger son, born in 1805. The bible's earliest entry is dated 1700. Trevor GIBBONS also has a diary for the years 1761-2, kept by one Matthew GIBBONS. He is a direct ancestor of both Trevor and my wife.

Irene and I have probably met more new relatives through just *one* of her lines than all the rest of our families put together. For several years, we have been tracing the descendants of her direct ancestor Robert JENKINSON, a Filey fisherman who died in 1808. We found that virtually all the JENKINSONs in Scarborough, Filey and Bridlington are his descendants, though of course they didn't know it. We wrote a book on the family and included a family tree which, though going down only to about 1900, had hundreds of names on it. Most of his descendants, of course, do not have the name JENKINSON, since daughters, granddaughters and so on lose the name at marriage. We reckon he has substantially over 1,000 living descendants today. Scores of them are still fishermen.

So, the direction of your investigation is a personal choice. The delightful thing about every piece of research is that your family tree will be unique to you, your brothers, sisters and all of your descendants. You will discover something about your own genetic ingredients, you should learn more history than most textbooks can teach, but above all you may come to sense the elusive bonds which tie us all to the dead and to the unborn.

But there are risks. In 1985, Bob and Nina SMITH were in their 70s when crime writer Jonathan GOODMAN contacted them, having traced them through their mother's 1967 death certificate. The brother and sister had no idea that the mother they had known as Ethel NEAVE had in fact been Ethel LE NEVE, mistress of the 1910 North London murderer Dr Hawley CRIPPEN. Acquitted of being an accessory, she had cosmeticised her true identity and begun a fresh life after he was hanged. You may not find so notorious a wife-killer in your own family - but this story is an eerie reminder of how a little delving can conjure up cold and unwelcome intrusions from the distant past.

2 PEDIGREE CHARTS AND DISPLAY METHODS

Your first step is to set down what you already know. Most people start with a standard pedigree chart, A4 sized (ie 11.7" by 8.3"). These can be bought quite cheaply (see p12) but it is quite easy to draft out a tree of your own, as I have done here (Figure 1).

These pedigree charts are the building blocks of your family tree, and you add to them as you collect additional information.

When I started, I was lucky - both my parents were alive, and could provide me with the names of their parents, and most of their grandparents.

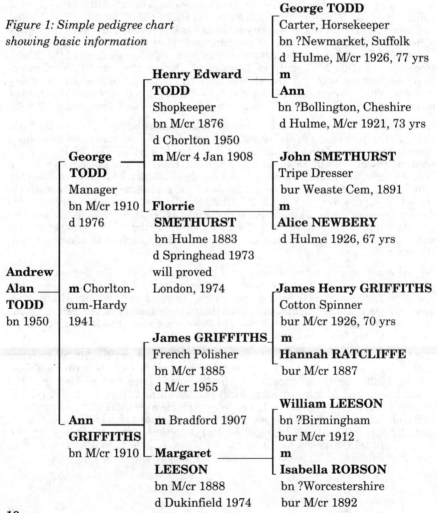

Figure 1: Simple pedigree chart showing basic information

George TODD
Carter, Horsekeeper
bn ?Newmarket, Suffolk
d Hulme, M/cr 1926, 77 yrs
m
Ann
bn ?Bollington, Cheshire
d Hulme, M/cr 1921, 73 yrs

Henry Edward TODD
Shopkeeper
bn M/cr 1876
d Chorlton 1950
m M/cr 4 Jan 1908

John SMETHURST
Tripe Dresser
bur Weaste Cem, 1891
m
Alice NEWBERY
d Hulme 1926, 67 yrs

George TODD
Manager
bn M/cr 1910
d 1976

Florrie SMETHURST
bn Hulme 1883
d Springhead 1973
will proved
London, 1974

Andrew Alan TODD
bn 1950

m Chorlton-cum-Hardy 1941

James Henry GRIFFITHS
Cotton Spinner
bur M/cr 1926, 70 yrs
m
Hannah RATCLIFFE
bur M/cr 1887

James GRIFFITHS
French Polisher
bn M/cr 1885
d M/cr 1955
m Bradford 1907

William LEESON
bn ?Birmingham
bur M/cr 1912
m
Isabella ROBSON
bn ?Worcestershire
bur M/cr 1892

Ann GRIFFITHS
bn M/cr 1910

Margaret LEESON
bn M/cr 1888
d Dukinfield 1974

10

On this simple direct line pedigree, notice four basic rules:

1) Males always go above their spouses.

2) Females are always known by their maiden surnames. Since my father, George TODD, did not know the maiden name of his grandmother, she had to go down (for the time being) simply as Ann. It would be confusing to call her Ann TODD, even though she was known as such for most of her life.

3) You must record your blood line. Step-parents cannot be recorded on this tree. Even if you do not wish to trace your grandfather's line because he deserted your grandmother at your father's birth to decamp with another woman, he must still appear on your pedigree. Think for the future. If, in a century's time, your great grandchildren find this piece of yellowing paper lying amongst your (hopefully uncleared) things, you would not want to mislead them.

4) These charts cannot show non-ancestral spouses. This is not because they are irrelevant - a large number of our ancestors were brought up by step-parents (in the mid-19th Century, about a third of all eight year olds had already lost a parent). Remarriage often followed bereavement with what we might now consider indecent haste. Economic necessity, not heartlessness, prompted this.

Similarly, simple direct ancestry trees have no space for brothers and sisters in any generation. These too are of crucial importance (naming patterns, for instance, carry clues from earlier generations). Methods of recording these non-ancestral relatives are considered later.

If you are able to progress immediately beyond the fourth generation (ie your great grandparents) you are lucky. Many people start their family history with no ancestors alive at all. Ironically, it often takes the death of a parent to inspire the first interest in his/her family origins. By then, you can quiz your key informant only at a seance.

Direct ancestry pedigree charts of all sizes are now widely available. Most provide space for the stock genealogical information shown on my chart on page 10. You should be able to discover dates of birth (bn) for ancestors born after 1837. Before that, parish registers (the staple diet of the family historian) give only dates of baptism (bpt). Similarly, distinguish between died (d) and buried (bur).

A4 pedigree charts are the most manageable size. They can be photocopied easily, so that a duplicate can be kept at the front of your research file for reference. Relatives, fellow researchers and family history society archives can each have a copy. This size often accommodates five generations - you on the left, your 16 great great grandparents on the far right. You can then start a new chart for each of the 16 as your research progresses.

Large charts, displaying eight generations or more, can be bought, but the mathematics of ancestry leave little space for your more remote forbears. One solution is the pedigree wheel - the circumference obligingly expands as you move outwards through the generations, but so do the embarrassingly empty segments. One of my great grandfathers has eluded investigation and his blank eighth is a tiresome reminder of my failure.

Your ambition will probably be to fill an entire wall with a giant pedigree, but family group sheets must come first. Pioneered by the Mormon Church, they are now available in various styles, usually A4 sized. All let you show one ancestral couple and their children, together with dates of birth, marriage and death (Figure 3, p15). They can be completed as you progress through each stage of your research - they are satisfying, visual milestones which can be stored in loose leafed files so that more can always be added. Once you have mastered the layout, you can draw up your own on plain paper. Creative use of photocopies of photographs, documents, maps and signatures can elevate them into works of art. A file full makes an ideal family present; and organisations like the Society of Genealogists (*) and the Mormon Church (*) welcome such material for their own extensive collections. Wide distribution ensures survival.

My wife and I designed many types of display and record charts for our own use, and eventually decided to print them for sale to other researchers. A catalogue of these products can be obtained from us in return for a first class stamp - Allen & Todd, 9-11 Square Street, Ramsbottom, Bury, Lancashire BL0 9BE. Examples in this book are the Family Group Sheet (p15), the Questionnaire (p17), the Census Record Sheet (p49) and the Family Census Record (p50).

Our packs of Personal Details Sheets are probably the biggest seller. These allow you to bring together onto a single A4 sheet all the information you have on each relative. They are biographical summaries. Your file full of these may, one day, be the most valuable legacy you pass on to your descendants.

If you do go on to unearth some family history, you will probably find that a passing curiosity escalates into a lifetime's addiction. It is a pastime which fills files fast! It took me many years of scruffy note-taking before I began to deal with *the* crucial issue for the family historian - how to record your findings in such a way that in time to come, you, or your grieving offspring, will be able to understand your notes and charts. And in 2094, it is important that your descendants will understand what you've found out about the family's past, so that they don't have to repeat all the work you've already done. (Don't forget that they will have a lot more to research than you did - for at every generation between you and them, their ancestral portfolio will have doubled!) With this in mind, I have distilled from many years of untidiness what I hope will be a compendium of useful tips in my *Basic Record Keeping for Family Historians: an Antidote to Chaos . . . and no computers!* Details are in the catalogue, mentioned above.

For those who have come to terms with personal computers, Hawgood (1) is an introduction to their use for filing, organising, sorting, searching and presenting data from family research.

Finally, whatever chart you fill in, be honest. You will be told information which is not certain fact - somebody's date of birth for example. Either put a question mark before such 'facts' or write them in pencil, to indicate their provisional nature.

FURTHER READING*

1 David Hawgood, *Computers for Family History - An Introduction* (4th ed, 1992)

* Many of the titles included in each chapter's *Further Reading* section can be obtained direct from us - for details, see the insert in the centre of this book.

3 INFORMATION FROM RELATIVES

Let's face it, we don't have any choice about the clutch of relatives into which we are born; so it's not surprising that as soon as we are old enough to exercise choice we keep most of them at a safe distance. No wonder we soon lose touch. The stream of life pushes families apart. Brothers may be close, but their children won't be, and their grandchildren probably won't even know each other's names. And of course, every family has a feud smouldering somewhere.

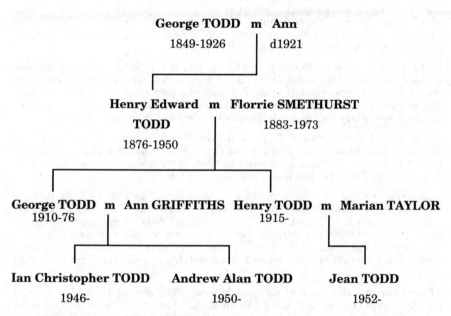

Figure 2: Pedigree showing direct line, siblings and one collateral line

This was my own TODD family as far as I knew it. My kinship horizon probably accorded with most people's - I knew about my grandparents, my uncle, and my cousin, but brothers and sisters further back were shadowy, nameless figures. Small dots of information had survived about George TODD (1849-1926), my great grandfather. He came from Newmarket to Manchester, he was a carter and later a horsekeeper (he even had a horsey smell). A photograph of him and his wife had hung on my grandparents' wall for years, but had disappeared long ago. One of my greatest initial disappointments was that I would never know what George and Ann looked like.

Figure 2 is a basic line pedigree. You will find it helpful to draw up trees like this in the course of your research - they, like pedigree charts, can be copied and sent to relatives. Simple rules to note are:

1) Don't crowd it with too much detail - its primary purpose is to show relationships and lifespans.

2) George TODD (born 1910) was older than his brother Henry so he goes to the left.

3) Always show children descending from a marriage sign (m). This becomes important where people married more than once - children must connect up with the right parents.

McLaughlin (2) is a very cheap guide to the techniques of drafting pedigrees.

My grandfather, Henry Edward TODD, was a quiet, mild man. His wife, Florrie, was somewhat different, and successfully entered into dispute with most living creatures that she encountered. After this marriage, our branch of the TODD family retreated into a separate line of evolution, and the rest of the clan enjoyed over half a century of uninterrupted tranquility until I set about rediscovering them. By quizzing my father, and later my Uncle Henry, I established that my grandfather was actually the eldest of five children.

I set these out on our A4 family group sheet (Figure 3, p15). As you exhume your ancestral families, you will want to record all the children. You can show up to six on these sheets (enough space for most modern families) and by leaving spaces you can neatly show smaller broods. We also produce sheets for up to 12 children, necessary for the larger families of the pre-20th Century period.

All four of Henry Edward TODD's brothers and sisters married and had children. Alfred had seven, Edith Annie three, Mary Elizabeth ('Polly') one, and Lily two. So my father had 13 cousins on his father's side, none of whom I'd ever met. Most of them had lost touch with one another.

Years ago, we had had Christmas cards from my father's Aunt Polly in New Zealand, but the contact had long since lapsed. In the late 1970s, when I became interested in my family, I wrote to the old address. Polly's daughter replied, and acted as a scribe for her mother - and I got several pages of family history, including the full names of the parents of George TODD and Ann GATENBY, his wife. Also, I was given some old addresses, notably Alfred's son, Frank (then in his 70s).

I have to be brutally frank - I was just in time. Polly died in 1980, at the age of 96, the last of George and Ann's five children. The moral 'never put off until tomorrow what you can do today' is more relevant to family history than to any other human activity.

Once having made a contact, addresses of other cousins followed, and I visited quite a number. Where possible, I record my relatives on cassette tape recorder - this will preserve their words for half a century or more on magnetic tape. (In my experience, people are flattered when you ask to record what they say but I have once resorted to clandestine recording.)

You do need a clear idea of what you want to know from someone. For this reason, I designed a questionnaire which I could use to record virtually every possible piece of useful information about any one ancestor. I could also send it by post to the more distant informants.

On page 17 you can see the outcome of my interview with Frank TODD, my father's first cousin. I asked him, in this instance, about his father, Alfred TODD, but could have done the same for his grandparents, George and Ann. By concentrating on one person at a time, the questionnaire should prevent confusion between different relatives on the part of the interviewee.

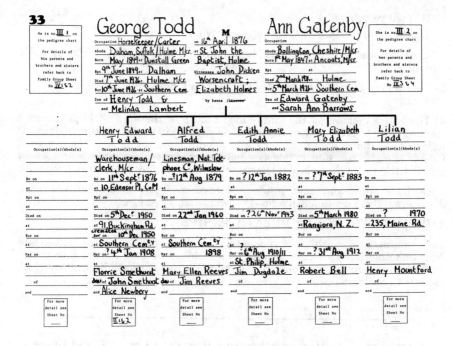

Figure 3: Family Group Sheet (reduced from A4)

Collect information about all the children that an ancestor had, not only the ancestral one. This theme of researching the family rather than the individual will crop up regularly in this book.

Families are like bagatelles - different pieces of information are remembered down different branches of the family, just as the balls can roll down the table in many directions. This, apart from intrinsic social benefits, is the reason for contacting as many cousins as possible.

The questionnaire is very detailed - but it will unearth some vital clues if you are lucky. (In this case, Frank, who died in 1985, was probably the last man alive to have memories of an ancestral photograph of an American Civil War soldier - a unique piece of information which helped to account for my great great grandfather's disappearance from his family in the 1850s.)

Some other hints on questioning your relatives:

1) Record family traditions meticulously. They will be grossly exaggerated or ridiculously simplistic, but usually contain a speck of truth. (One researcher relates how a piece of family lore referring to 'a red man' and 'a black man' turned out, on investigation, to relate to a late 19th Century ancestor's move from iron mining in the Forest of Dean to coal mining in South Yorkshire.) Bear in mind how quickly the simplest tale gets distorted when it is passed on orally.

2) Suggest major events as reference points for your informant:

'He died years ago.'

'Would that be before the Second World War?'

'Oh no ... it was right at the end ... he fell under a tram whilst celebrating on VJ night.'

3) Get them in pairs if you can. Arguments about dates and names lead to more accuracy.

4) The oldest member of the family may not know the most. Old people may recount more to their very young grandchildren than to their adult children. It follows that the middle aged may know more than the aged. Also, in-laws, friends, neighbours and employees may have soaked up more *controversial* family tittle-tattle than close relatives - the children may never have been told.

5) Go back when you have progressed further. Feed back what you have discovered; this may unleash a flood of long submerged facts.

THE TERMINOLOGY OF RELATIONSHIPS

Take yourself. Then think of your aunt - her children are your first cousins. Now imagine that your first cousin has a child - that child is your first cousin once removed. As you age, your first cousin may have grandchildren. They will be your first cousins twice removed, and you are the same to them.

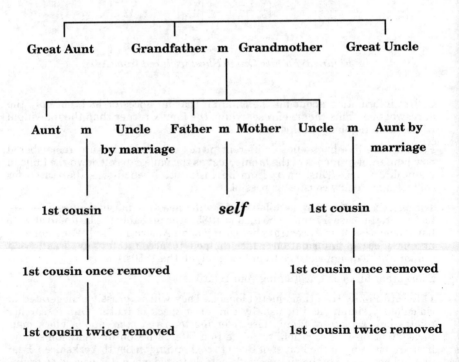

Figure 4: Egocentric kinship

25 | **INFORMATION GIVEN BY** Frank Todd

on the 6ᵗʰ Oct 1979 (date) at 78, Albert St., Ramsbottom, Bury (address)

about Alfred Todd , his/her father

(Interviewed by Andrew A. Todd)

NAME	What was his/her full name?	Alfred Todd
	Did he/she go under any other name, like a familiar name?	Alf
BURIAL	Where was he/she buried/cremated?	buried Southern Cemetery, Manchester
	Was he/she buried as C of E, Methodist, R C etc?	Methodist section
	When was he/she buried/cremated?	January 1960 How old was he/she? 81
	Is there a gravestone?	Grave nº K1105 – has stone
DEATH	Where did he/she die?	Manchester
	When did he/she die?	22ⁿᵈ January 1960
	What was his/her cause of death?	
	Did he/she leave a will?	
BIRTH	Where was he/she born?	Manchester
	When was he/she born?	'Official' date was 25ᵗʰ August; real date 12ᵗʰ Aug 1879
	What was the full name of his/her father?	George Todd
	What was the full name, and maiden name of his/her mother?	Ann Gatenby
	Where was he/she baptised?	

SCHOOLS/ EDUCATION	Places and dates of his/her education:	**RELIGION**	Did he/she attend church/chapel regularly?
			Did he/she belong to any religious organisations like t[...]
JOBS	Occupation · date(s)	**PERSONAL**	Can you give a description of him/her - height, build, [...]
	Linesman & exchange operator · early 190[0]		Heavy build, grey hair in old age, wo[...]
			What hobbies/pastimes/interests did he/she have?
			Liked a drink
		RELATIVES	Were there any relatives that he/she visited/kept in to[...]
			Aunt Lizzie (née Gatenby) Holmes used to visit, in Frank's childhood
			Were there any family photographs? One on the
MILITARY	Did he/she serve in the army, navy, or R A F?		soldier in American Civil War unif[...]
CAREER	What regiment(s), ship(s), or squadron(s) was		Was there a family bible?
	Manchester Regiment		Who has it now?
	Service No? 4434 Any medal[s]		Were there any family traditions/legends? Todd f[...]
	Where did he/she serve, and when?		according to Alfred – lost their land
	Palestine until the end of t[...] wounded three times, once in		Ann Gatenby (said Alfred) came

		MARRIAGE(S)	His/her spouse's full name	date
ADDRESSES	Please list the place(s) he/she lived, with d[...]	1st	Mary Ellen Reeves	c1898
	172, York St., Hulme, M/cr – [...]	2nd		
		3rd		

CHILDREN	Child's full name	child's date of birth	child'
	Name of other parent	...and date of death	...and
1st	Edie	19ᵗʰ Oct 1899	Ma
	Mary Ellen (Reeves)		sti
2nd	Ernest	19ᵗʰ Aug 1901	Ma
	Mary Ellen (Reeves)		
3rd	James Henry	? Aug 1903-4	Ma
	Mary Ellen (Reeves)	June 1970	
4th	Lily	16ᵗʰ June 1907	

Newmarket, Suffolk – c1919 cousin there, from rheumat[...]

Figure 5: Portions of the two-sided Questionnaire (reduced from A4)

Now imagine both yourself and your first cousin with a child each. Their relationship to one another is second cousin.

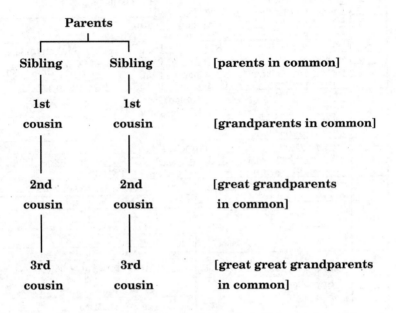

Figure 6: Degrees of cousinship

The cardinal number - 1st, 2nd, 3rd and so on, is determined by the number of generations you must go back to find the marriage from which you both descend. It is unusual for people to know collateral relatives descending from marriages which took place more than a century ago. Second cousins are about the limit of most human knowledge (or interest). This is partly because they are so common - if every family from which you descend has had two children, and your collateral families have been equally uniform, you will have 16 second cousins. But since families were usually far larger than this until well into the present century, the numbers escalate rapidly.

One of the headiest experiences that awaits you, as a family historian, is the 99% chance that you will, through your hobby, meet new relatives. The nearer the connecting marriage is to you in time, the greater the number of shared genes - and the better the chance that you will see (or hear) familiar characteristics. There is, however, a special thrill in meeting distant relatives where the connecting marriage occurred perhaps in 1854, or 1793 or even earlier. The chances of this happening increase with remarkable speed the further back you go, and the more lines you develop.

A final word about cousins. You may get something more tangible from them than factual information or family tradition. My father's cousin, Frank TODD, had a photograph of his grandmother, Ann GATENBY (my great grandmother) whose likeness I had given up as lost. His daughter and granddaughters, incidentally, are uncannily similar to her in their features. Another cousin had a small photograph of George TODD, my great grandfather, complete with horse and coal cart!

Many family photographs were lent to me as a result of my genealogical nosings. Together, they threw up a chilling phenomenon - the TODD nose! It would appear that for unknown generations the TODDs have sported this prominent heirloom. (Having inspected these photographs, my wife also pointed out, rather insensitively, the 'frog eyes' which lurk submerged in the TODD gene pool.)

Equally unnerving was the only surviving photograph of my great grandfather, George. He stands in some Manchester coalyard and grins at me across 90 years - yet his grin and pose are so familiar, for my brother Ian has them exactly.

Drawers and cupboards in any house are often replete with family memorabilia. This is yet another good reason for unearthing as many cousins (and therefore as many drawers and cupboards) as possible.

MISSING RELATIVES

It is possible that all you know of a cousin is a very old address. It is worth sending this, together with his/her full name, and approximate age (or date of birth if known) and last known marital status to:-

> Contributions Agency,
>
> Special Section A, CACO 101B,
>
> Department of Social Security,
>
> Longbenton, Newcastle upon Tyne NE98 1YX
>
> Tel 06451 55051 (BT Local Call rates)

The department won't disclose the address, but they will, for 'welfare purposes', forward a letter from you to the most recent address in their records. In practice, you need to establish that contact is necessary on account of serious illness or death. Since both are certain to have occurred at some time in your immediate family's recent past, it takes only a little creativity on your part to convince the Agency that they should forward your letter. Unfortunately, standard replies from the DSS like 'We have been unable to trace a National Insurance account for this person' or 'We have no record of this person's present address' tell you little.

Ironically, you can trace the whereabouts of a 19th Century ancestor more easily than those of a living but lost cousin. Given that important documents or information may be held by such relatives, the problem is of great interest to family historians, and is well treated in Rogers (3). An index of missing live persons is maintained by the Society of Genealogists (*).

Your lost relative may have died in a World War II bombing raid - the Commonwealth War Graves Commission (*) will release information from *Civilian War Dead* on any of the 66,375 Britons listed. This gives date and place of death (19,000 in London) *or* of injury and death; next of kin; and age of the person.

FURTHER READING

2 Eve McLaughlin, *Laying out a Pedigree* (McLaughlin Guides, 1988)

3 Colin Rogers, *Tracing Missing Persons : An Introduction to Agencies, Methods and Sources in England and Wales* (Manchester University Press, 1986)

4 AROUND THE HOUSE

In 1977, I received an invitation to a friend's wedding. Should one of his descendants chance upon a fading copy in a drawer many years from now, what a wealth of pointers it would provide for his family's history. He would have the names of an ancestral couple; the bride's parents and their likely religion; their address; and the date and place of the marriage (Figure 7).

There are dozens of documents and artefacts lying around relatives' houses which can provide equally valuable information.

With luck, each one should furnish you with ancestral minutiae from two or more of these categories:

FULL NAMES ADDRESSES DATES OCCUPATIONS RELATIONSHIPS

Human documentary ephemera, so crucial to ancestral research, falls into three groupings:

PERSONAL ITEMS

Funeral cards have name, address and age of deceased, with location of burial.

Family bibles may carry a string of dates of birth, marriage and death on a flyleaf, or between the Old and New Testaments. Traditionally a wedding present to a bride, they were often entrusted to daughters and are soon 'lost' to the male line of the family. They are worth moving heaven and earth to locate. A girl I taught found a single flyleaf at the bottom of a wardrobe - it took her family back to a marriage of around 1810.

Birthday cards are especially useful when dated. Books were commonly inscribed and presented to punctilious members by schools and religious organisations. They may be a clue to ages and religious persuasions. Family baptisms may be found in the church's registers.

Photographs are most useful if endorsed with their subjects' names. Inevitably, though, you will have the disagreeable experience of finding some anonymous Victorian face peering out of one at you, unknown to any living person. Hawk it round all your cousins (they may have the same one, and be able to identify it). Try dating it from a book of costumes - the age of the person, the address

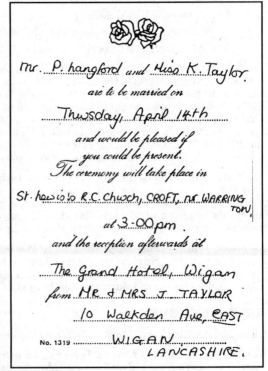

Figure 7: *Family ephemera - a 1977 invitation*

20

of the photographer's studio and the photograph's current resting place could suggest an identity. Military men are more readily identifiable in reference books on uniforms and medals. For dating by photographic type and costume see Steel and Taylor (6) or Lansdell (4). Your local family history society's expert may help you. (Tapping into expertise like this can produce miraculous results - I know a retired sea captain who, shown an unidentified harbour snap, could interpret the tide, the type of boats and their rig, the seasonal fishing gear and the fishermen to pin down the scene almost to the hour and the day on which it had been taken.)

Save your descendants such agonising by endorsing all photographs with the name and date of the subject - in pencil, since ink may eventually penetrate through to the print.

Letters and postcards - my wife, Irene, unearthed a cache of postcards from drawers and niches in her mother's house. They spanned the first half of this century and enabled us to piece together the childhood of her father's cousins Percy and Reggie, and their premature deaths (from tuberculosis and wounds from the Great War respectively) in 1916 and 1922. The cards helped us to identify a number of family photographs. A card written in Burton-on-Trent cemetery in 1945 reported the location and plot numbers of two family graves. People who sent some of these cards may eventually prove to be cousins or in-laws. Yet even if letters and postcards don't expand your tree backwards very far, they resurrect their authors more efficiently than most family ephemera.

Diaries and account books - nothing revitalises the past like a diary. I once spent an hour, effectively in the 1790s, whilst reading in Leicestershire Record Office the diary and account book of a farmer, John SIMMONDS. My father kept a very detailed account book - it itemised disbursements for anything from his mother's medicines (ending abruptly in 1973 at her death) to his wife's housekeeping money and my weekly spends.

Address books - numerous relatives may figure in these.

Birthday books - a calendar of family birthdays for the absent minded. Rare.

STATE ISSUED ITEMS

Birth, marriage and death certificates - fortunately, the items most likely to be hoarded. Alien surnames on yellowing 19th Century certificates will be your first encounter with long forgotten ancestral lines. Nothing is so annoying as spending £5.00 at a register office for a copy of your great grandfather's birth certificate when the copy he used to verify his pension rights has all the time been lying undisturbed at the bottom of granny's drawer.

School leaving certificates were proof that somebody could be legally employed. Compulsory elementary education began in most areas in 1870, and everywhere by 1880. The minimum school leaving age was 10, from 1893 11 and from 1899 12. In 1900, local authorities could raise it to 14, and after 1918 had to. It was 15 by 1947, and 16 in 1974.

School reports - another clue to schools attended. Registers of admissions (at the school or in the local authority archives) should give date of birth, address and names of parents.

National Health Service medical cards - every living person was given an identity card and number in September 1939, at the outbreak of World War II.

This became each individual's NHS number when the system was created after the War. Since then, every newly registered child and immigrant registering with an NHS doctor has received one. The four letters in the number provide a key to abode - about as precise as a modern postcode.

National Insurance documents, Driver's Licences - all carry names and addresses. Like the NHS numbers, there is currently no public access to the central bank of records, although date of birth is only crudely coded in the modern Driver's DVLC Number.

Before World War II, full name, rank, unit and military number appeared on the rim of *medals*. Bronze plaques, individually named, were issued to the next of kin of all men killed in the Great War.

Discharge papers carry the same information as on medals, with year of birth and years of service. Of the many official papers accumulated by a soldier, these are most likely to survive, since they proved he was not a deserter (see Figure 8).

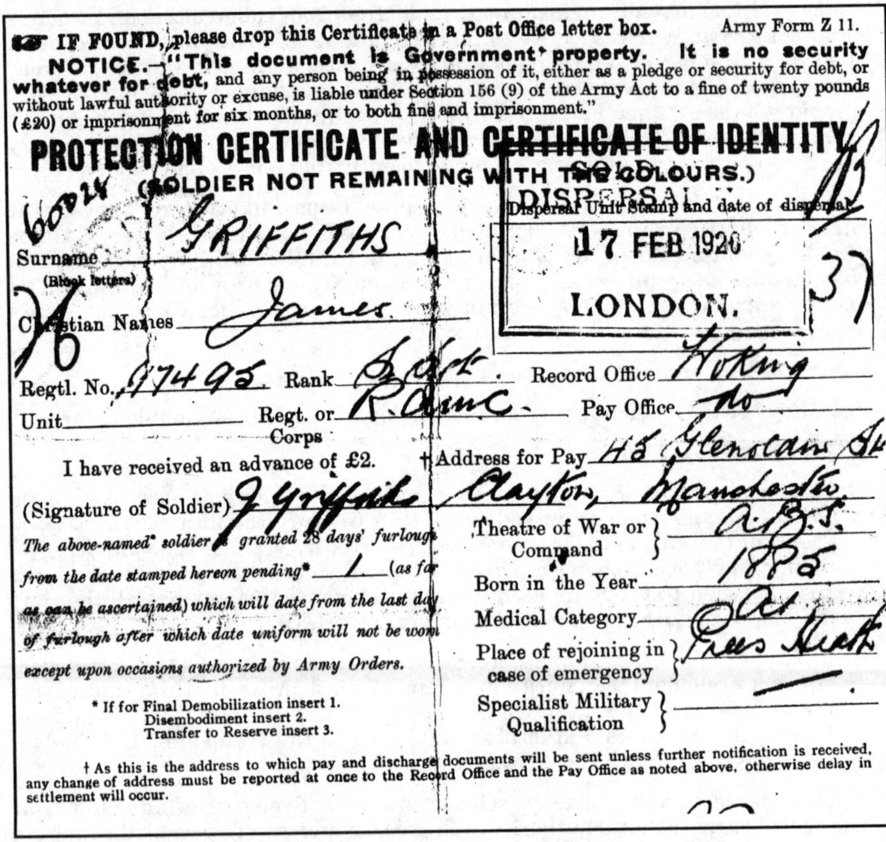

IF FOUND, please drop this Certificate in a Post Office letter box. Army Form Z 11.

NOTICE.—"This document is Government property. It is no security whatever for debt, and any person being in possession of it, either as a pledge or security for debt, or without lawful authority or excuse, is liable under Section 156 (9) of the Army Act to a fine of twenty pounds (£20) or imprisonment for six months, or to both fine and imprisonment."

PROTECTION CERTIFICATE AND CERTIFICATE OF IDENTITY

(SOLDIER NOT REMAINING WITH THE COLOURS.)

Dispersal Unit Stamp and date of dispersal: DISPERSAL 17 FEB 1920 LONDON.

Surname (Block letters): GRIFFITHS

Christian Names: James

Regtl. No. 97495 Rank Record Office

Unit Regt. or Corps Pay Office

I have received an advance of £2. †Address for Pay

(Signature of Soldier) J Griffiths

The above-named soldier is granted 28 days' furlough from the date stamped hereon pending** 1 *(as far as can be ascertained) which will date from the last day of furlough after which date uniform will not be worn except upon occasions authorized by Army Orders.*

Theatre of War or Command

Born in the Year 1885

Medical Category

Place of rejoining in case of emergency

Specialist Military Qualification

* If for Final Demobilization insert 1.
Disembodiment insert 2.
Transfer to Reserve insert 3.

† As this is the address to which pay and discharge documents will be sent unless further notification is received, any change of address must be reported at once to the Record Office and the Pay Office as noted above, otherwise delay in settlement will occur.

Figure 8: Part of a Demobilisation Certificate, giving army number, unit, home address and year of birth

PAPERS FROM OTHER ORGANISATIONS

Grave ownership papers are invaluable keys to any family graves (see p26).

Newspaper cuttings may log retirements, funerals, obituaries, veterans' parades, royal visits or crimes which involved your ancestors actively or passively.

Wage slips, bills, receipts, business cards are clues to occupations.

Wills, letters of administration - survivals in family possession will be executors' copies.

Insurance policies, including *burial society membership documents*, will at least provide names and addresses.

Trades union and friendly society papers such as membership cards, subscription cards and receipts may lead to references to an ancestor in the organisation's records (see Rogers **(5)** pp 30-40).

This list is the tip of a large iceberg. Collect everything. Don't discriminate - items may tie in later. Try to get photocopies of family documents which are not in your possession.

This collecting process can go on as long as you keep locating new relations. Sooner or later, though, you should have enough biographical information to venture beyond your family and house.

It would take several lifetimes to familiarise yourself with every class of record which could contain references to your ancestors. Fortunately, most people can compile respectable family histories back to the early 19th Century by using only a readily accessible handful.

Chronologically, your ancestors were closest to you at their deaths. This obvious circumstance accounts for the first port of call in our search for helpful records...

OBITUARY

MISS I LEESON

THE funeral service of Miss Isabella Leeson has taken place at Hale Cemetery.

Miss Leeson of 52, Lloyd Street, Altrincham, who leaves a sister Dorothy, was born in Bradford, Manchester, in 1900.

She came to Altrincham in 1901 and had lived at 52, Lloyd Street for the past 70 years. From 1919 to 1939 she was employed by A. and B. Laundry, Moss Lane, Altrincham, as a finery ironer.

For the last 12 years before her retirement she was employed by J. S. Kinsey, Ashley Road, Hale, as a cabinet maker.

Miss Leeson, who had been almost blind all her life, was keen on knitting and crochet work in spite of her handicap. She was a lifelong member of Hale Road Baptist Church, having been baptised there when she was 17. After her retirement she joined Altrincham Darby and Joan Club and was a member for 15 years.

The service was conducted by the Rev W. G. Barnes, a former minister of the Church.

Arrangements were by A. B. Brookes and Sons Ltd.

Figure 9: A 1974 newscutting giving much biographical detail

FURTHER READING

4 Avril Lansdell, *Fashion a la Carte: A Study of Fashion through Cartes- de-Visite* (Shire, 1985)

5 Colin Rogers, *The Family Tree Detective* (Manchester University Press, 1986)

6 Don Steel & Lawrence Taylor (ed), *Family History in Focus* (Lutterworth Press, 1985)

5 CEMETERY RECORDS

By 1851, more people in Britain lived in towns and cities than lived in the countryside. It is no coincidence, therefore, that from the 1850s to about the 1960s (when cremation became 'popular') municipal cemeteries were the last resting place of most people. Before the 1850s, virtually everybody ended up in the graveyard of a parish church or chapel. Some non-Anglican sects also had licences to bury - Quaker burial grounds date back to the 17th Century.

Before the 1850s, therefore, the only record of burial will probably be the entry in the church or chapel register. Gravestones with monumental inscriptions may also survive there. (Where a body was unavailable for burial - in the case of disappearance at sea, for example - no entry in the register will be found, although the death may be commemorated on the family gravestone.)

Many ancient parish churchyards have been consecrated for burial for a millenium or more. In such a vast span of generations, even a small parish could furnish numerous corpses. The yard at Heptonstall, a chapelry in the ancient parish of Halifax, is reputed to contain 100,000 bodies in only a few acres. Visitors to old churchyards will have noticed how they are physically raised up above the level of surrounding streets or lanes. The reason is obvious!

Urban centres suffered pressure on burial space first, and in some cases parish churches purchased additional burial ground at some distance from the original yard. In the 1820s and 1830s, private enterprise provided cemeteries in the largest towns and cities, and non-conformists often opted for burial there, in preference to interment at a parish church, even though fees might have to be paid to both.

After 1852 (London) and 1853 (the rest of the country) burial boards could be set up to lay out public (ie municipal) cemeteries. These were on outskirts of towns, where land was cheaper and health hazards reduced. It is at this time that the burial registers of many urban parish churches come to an abrupt end, with only the occasional reopening, by special authorisation, of a family grave for a new addition. Burials in rural, less crowded parish churchyards continue to this day. C of E yards have, since 1880, been open for non-Anglican interments.

Brooks (7) lists the larger British cemeteries, with dates, and number of burials.

LOCATION OF CEMETERY RECORDS

Once full, **private cemeteries** ceased trading, and their yards were often greened over. After 1906, a record had to be kept, by law, of inscriptions on such cleared gravestones. This, along with the cemetery's burial registers, can usually be found at the appropriate county record office, or local authority archives.

Responsibility for all **municipal cemeteries** has been in the hands of district authorities in England and Wales since 1974. These are the local authorities below the level of county councils, and have titles such as East Staffordshire District Council, Derby City Council or Scarborough Borough Council. In metropolitan areas, they are metropolitan district or metropolitan borough councils, and in London the boroughs. District and Island authorities have this responsibility in Scotland, and districts/boroughs in Northern Ireland. Each of these local authorities has a department which administers its cemeteries. This may be called simply *Cemeteries and Crematoria, Parks and Recreational Services*, or, even more ironically, *Parks and Leisure Department*! The address can be found in the local authority's block entry in the telephone directory.

If you live away from the area, you can find all the country's telephone directories in any library, or in a central post office.

In most libraries, you will also find Godwin's *Concise Guide to Local Authorities in England & Wales* (1974). It has county maps showing the boundaries of the present district/borough authorities and principal large towns. An alphabetical list of authorities indicates their constituent parts (pre-1974 urban and rural districts, and boroughs) together with the address of their headquarters.

```
Manchester City Council—contd.
  Recreational Services Dept—contd.
    Parks & Cemeteries,
      Offices Town Hall 2.............................061-236 3377
      Cemeteries & Crematorium,
        Blackley Cem.& Crematorium 9..............061-740 2523
        Do.............................................061-740 5359
        Gorton Cem, Thornwood Av 18...............061-223 0368
        Phillps Park Cem, Hulme Hall La 10........061-223 0018
        Southern Cem, Barlow Moor Rd 21..........061-881 2208
```

Figure 10: A local authority block entry in the telephone directory

The local authority department is usually the best place to start your enquiry, since they will know the whereabouts of records of their cemeteries. Increasingly, the older records are moved away from the cemetery offices - into the department itself or into the local authority archives. Cemetery records are now rarely available for public inspection. The staff will do a search, often for a fee. So it makes sense to have some idea of the date of death, and if possible, the religious denomination of the deceased. When making a postal enquiry, it is best to enclose an SAE.

RECORDS ASSOCIATED WITH MUNICIPAL CEMETERIES

1) The Burial Register

Below is a 20th Century example from Philip's Park Cemetery, Manchester:

No	Date	Name	Age	Rank or Profession	Abode	Parish or district	Mode of burial	Section	No	Minister
103967	4th Nov 1912	William Leeson	68	Watchman	140 Harold St	Bradford	Single	D	436	Edwin Jones

The register is a chronological record of burials. The running number (103,967) gives some idea of this cemetery's popularity! (This makes it necessary to have some notion about the date of death, to within about five years, the usual span that staff will search.) Earlier registers are rarely as detailed. Separate sections, and registers (often termed *Consecrated*) were kept for Anglicans. Roman Catholics were buried and registered in separate sections. *Non-Conformists* is the umbrella term for Methodists, Baptists and the rest - they are in a third register. So, you must search all three if you aren't sure of religious denomination.

A grave usually had six occupants (four in hard ground) though more could be accommodated if children were interred. A *common* or *single* plot was filled by bodies in order of arrival. Often called paupers' graves, they simply represented the cheapest type of funeral. Common graves in early cemeteries could be big - 20 foot deep 'pit burials' were known in London, whilst Ardwick had 30 footers.

Many people were particular about their partners in death, and families often bought *private* graves (sometimes known as *freehold* plots). Members of one family could then be interred together, over a period of many decades. Often, the grave number was included in the burial entry.

2) The Graves Book and Order Book

To keep track of how full any private grave was getting, the cemetery authorities summarised the interments in each plot in *graves books*. Detailed graves books for common graves are rare, since these plots would be filled quickly.

Order books may begin in the late 19th Century, and contain the administrative detail that was necessary to process each burial - name of deceased, age, address, date and time of burial, 'reopening' and burial fee, and, usefully, name and address of who paid them, although this might be the undertaker.

It follows that if you can locate one burial in a private grave, the graves book will give you the names of other members of the family. They may belong to earlier generations, and may have died a century before. Details of their interments should then be followed up in the burial register and order books. Remember that the whole point of buying the freehold of a private grave was to ensure that the family would stay together. So, no matter what the surnames of the occupants may be, there is a 95% chance that they are all related - somehow. You can expect to find a wife's parents there, or perhaps daughters under their married names.

It should be stressed that churches and chapels, as opposed to cemeteries, rarely have records of interment other than the register of burials. Very occasionally, the entries include a *grave number* (eg 27 46 3) - several apparently unrelated entries can therefore be identified as burials in one plot, probably a family grave. Some churches and chapels do have *grave plans* or *grave occupancy books*, but these rarely predate the 19th Century.

3) Burial Plot Deeds

When a private plot was sold by the burial board, a deed would be handed over to the buyer, as a receipt of payment and as proof of ownership. These useful documents often lie unrecognised and undisturbed for decades, in a drawer or cupboard. Since they pinpoint the plot exactly, it is simple to write to the district authority in whose territory the cemetery now lies. Ask for details from the order books, and the burial register, of all the people buried in that plot. The original date of the deed will be of significance. It would be morbid to buy a grave unless someone in the family had died. Burial plot deeds, of courses, will be in private hands, where they survive, and not at the cemetery office.

4) Monumental Inscriptions

Private graves may have stones; common graves rarely do - but beware of *subscription* or *public inscription* graves - ie a common grave with a stone carrying just a list of names. (One researcher spent months fruitlessly tracing the names of people buried with her uncle before discovering that unrelated people could be commemorated on such gravestones.) Nevertheless, once you have a grave number, it is worth going to the cemetery to see if there is a stone.

Highgate, London; Southern, Manchester - these great city cemeteries stretch for hundreds of acres. There is little point in searching for great granddad's stone on the basis of directions like 'over by the gate, under a tree'. Even town cemeteries can be huge. In 1935, a local newspaper reported that Blackburn Cemetery could boast 150,000 occupants, a figure which actually exceeded the living population of the town. The cemetery may have a grave map or key to direct you to the grave. This is a good reason for going in office hours. A gravestone may name people not in that particular grave - war dead, or relatives who died abroad or far afield in other circumstances. Similarly, there is no guarantee that a stone will name everybody in the grave. Related families were sometimes buried in adjacent or nearby plots, though this was more usual in churchyards.

Ownership of a plot is not perpetual. You may visit the family grave to find it and its gravestone unrecognisably landscaped away. Old private cemeteries are most vulnerable - the vandalised Undercliffe Cemetery, Bradford, was sold in 1975 for £5.00 to a property 'developer' who joined in the process of desecration by bulldozing gravestones and using kerbstones for building material, until the site was rescued in 1985 by a trust. Nor is municipal control necessarily more enlightened, judging by the bizarre attempt of Westminster City Council in 1987 to sell three cemeteries to 'developers' for 5p each.

CREMATION

Cremation dates from 1884, but only accounted for more than 10,000 people a year after 1945. By 1992, the 221 crematoria in the UK were disposing of 75% of the nation's dead. Most are in local authority care and many adjoin existing cemeteries. Registers of cremations are kept, and plaques should survive.

WHICH CEMETERY OR GRAVEYARD?

In a large town, there may have been many possible burial places. How can you ascertain which one contains your ancestor? Death certificates won't tell you. So try looking for:

1) *burial plot deeds* - ask all the family (distant cousins included) if one survives.

2) *funeral cards* - note that these may also have been retained by family friends.

3) the *local newspaper* may include a death notice, or even an obituary, indicating where the funeral took place (see Chapter 8).

4) a *map*. Generally speaking, people are buried in the district where they live. (Non-ratepayers were often charged double.) But note ...

5) *earlier addresses*. A family often had church burial rights, or might have bought a private cemetery plot, in an area from which it had moved.

6) opening dates of local churches or cemeteries can be found in the introductory historical descriptions in a town's or city's *trade directories* of the 19th and early 20th Century (see Chapter 8).

7) seek *local knowledge*. Several years might have separated the closure of a town's old churchyard and the opening of its cemetery. Some obscure church or chapel might have filled this burial gap.

8) .. and don't forget to ask *relatives*. It could save you a long search.

FURTHER READING

7 Chris Brooks, *Mortal Remains: the History and Present State of the Victorian and Edwardian Cemetery* (Exeter, 1989)

6 CENSUS RETURNS

THE 1851 CENSUS

The returns of the 1851 census of England and Wales are probably the most valuable archive freely available to family historians in this country. They were opened for public research in 1912, despite the guarantee of a century's confidentiality to the 17,927,609 people whose personal details had been scrupulously collected by the census enumerators.

The householders' schedules had been distributed in the week prior to Sunday 30 March. Each head of household whether of house or tenement (ie a part of a house separately occupied) had to fill in his/her copy as closely as possible to midnight that day, 'under penalty in case of wilful deceit'. Figure 11 shows the questions that had to be answered for each person who was staying the night. The schedules issued in Scotland, where a census was held simultaneously, were almost identical.

Instructions to aid the householder were on the reverse. Schedules in Welsh were provided 'for the use of the poorer native population of Wales'.

The 1851 census was a mammoth undertaking - nearly seven million schedules were distributed that week, by thousands of enumerators. In all, nearly 40 tons of official stationery were used. Everybody was to be included. Every householder received (or should have received) a schedule, whether owner or tenant. Separate apartments, cellars or rooms were treated as distinct households if separately occupied. Boarders, lodgers and temporary visitors were to be enumerated at the place where they were that night. Members of the household who were absent were not to be included. In this way double counting was to be avoided, although there is some evidence that it did take place. Nightworkers and overnight travellers were to be treated as residents in the household at which they stopped the following morning. Some were enumerated on Euston station in the early hours of the 31st. Occupants of boats were

	LIST of the MEMBERS of this FAMILY, of VISITORS, and of SERVANTS who SLI				
	NAME AND SURNAME.	RELATION to Head of Family.	CONDITION.	SEX.	AGE [Last Birthday.]
	No Person absent on the Night of March 30th to be entered. ——— Write after the Name of the Head of the Family, the Names of his Wife, Children, and others of the same Surname; then Visitors, Servants, &c.	State whether Wife, Son, Daughter or other Relative, Visitor, or Servant.	Write "Married," "Widower," "Widow," or "Unmarried," against the Names of all Persons except Young Children.	Write "M" against Males, and "F" against Females.	For Infants under One Year, state the Age in Months, writing "Under 1 Month," "1 Month," "2 Months," &c.
1					
2					
3					
4					

28

enumerated at the wharves and docks at which they were berthed. People in charge of institutions such as workhouses, hospitals, barracks, prisons, boarding schools and lunatic asylums were given especially large schedules to record their inmates.

On 31 March, each enumerator visited all the households in his enumeration district to collect the schedules. If a form were blank (as many must have been, owing to illiteracy) he had to fill it in himself, taking down the required information from the verbal responses of the householder, or indeed from anybody who might be available in the house. Having collected the form, the enumerator wrote the address on its reverse side. Often this was simply the name of the village or hamlet.

Each enumerator copied the entries from these schedules into an enumerator's book, in the order that they had been distributed. Figure 12 shows an example.

To distinguish between different houses, he drew a thick line across the page under the name and relationship of the last inhabitant. If two or more families occupied the same building, he drew a shorter line under the first household. Such short lines are therefore evidence of multiple occupancy of a single house. It is very easy, even for experienced researchers, to mistake these short lines for full lines, and therefore miss a second (often related) household living in with an ancestral family.

Alongside each household, the enumerator entered in his book:

1) the schedule number in the first (narrow) column. Be careful not to confuse this with the house number, rarely given in 1851.

2) the address (from the reverse of the form) in the second column. A second schedule number appearing lower down the page but under the same address is an indication of multiple occupancy.

ABODE in this House on the NIGHT of SUNDAY, MARCH 30th.		
RANK, PROFESSION, or OCCUPATION.	WHERE BORN.	If Deaf-and-Dumb, or Blind.
e filling in this Column, you are *requested to read the* *nstructions on the other side.)*	Opposite the Names of those born in England, write the *County*, and *Town* or *Parish*. If born in Scotland, Ireland, the British Colonies, the East Indies, or in Foreign Parts, state the *Country*; in the last case, if a British Subject, add, "*British Subject*."	Write "*Deaf-and-Dumb*," or "*Blind*," opposite the Name of the Person.

Figure 11: The top portion of the 1851 householder's schedule - the full form had spaces for 15 people

At the beginning of his book, the enumerator wrote a geographical description of the boundary of his district naming the streets (or, in rural areas, farms, hamlets and villages) which he had covered (see Figure 15, pp40-1).

These books were then forwarded to the registrar, who might have dozens of enumerators within his registrar's sub-district.

He then passed them to the Superindent Registrar of the registration district. Finally the books for each of the 623 registration districts reached Somerset House in London (Figure 16, p42) the then General Register Office.

These English and Welsh enumeration books have been microfilmed, and are available for public scrutiny at no charge, and without a reader's ticket, in the Census Rooms of the Public Record Office (*). Copies have also been purchased by libraries and record offices throughout the country, local authorities naturally buying those microfilms which cover their own areas. It is therefore possible to look at a town's 1851 census returns locally, and at no cost (although a very small number of record offices do charge).

LATER CENSUSES

The 1851 census was the first to have collected so much information. Later 19th Century returns followed almost exactly the same format, except that there was an extra (narrow) column after the address. In this, a number 1 indicated the start of another house. The returns of 1861, 1871, 1881 and 1891 are open to public research in the same way as those of 1851. The hundred year rule is now strictly adhered to - the 1901 census becomes a public record in January 2002.

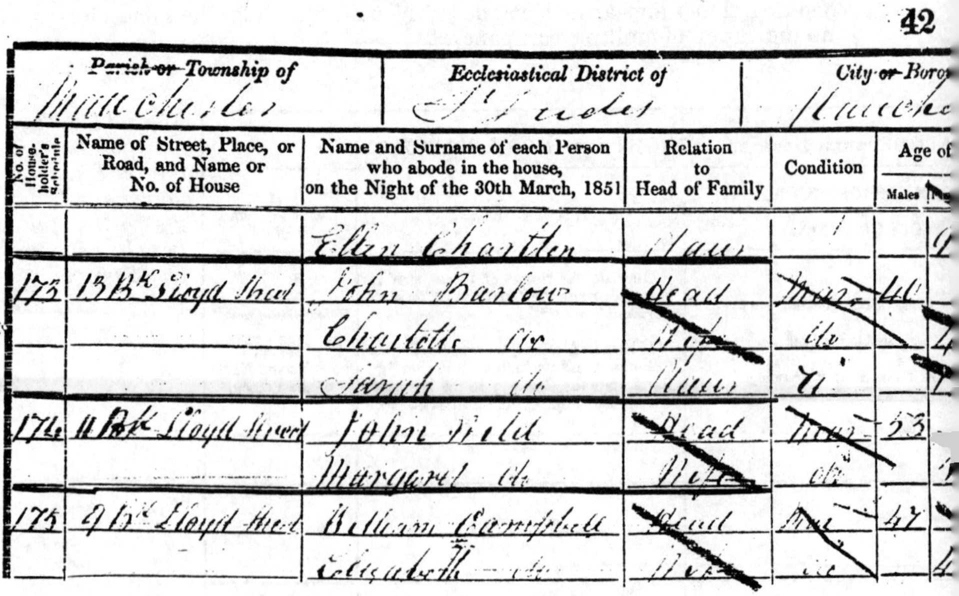

42

~~Parish or~~ Township of Manchester | Ecclesiastical District of St Judes | City ~~or Boro~~ Manche

No. of House-holder's Schedule	Name of Street, Place, or Road, and Name or No. of House	Name and Surname of each Person who abode in the house, on the Night of the 30th March, 1851	Relation to Head of Family	Condition	Age of Males
		Ellen Charlton	Daur		9
173	13 Bk Lloyd Street	John Barlow	Head	Mar	40
		Charlotte do	Wife	do	
		Sarah do	Daur	U	
174	11 Bk Lloyd Street	John Wild	Head	Mar	53
		Margaret do	Wife	do	
175	9 Bk Lloyd Street	William Campbell	Head	Mar	47
		Elizabeth do	Wife	do	

Figure 12: The top portion of a page of an 1851 enumerator's book.

A small difference in the enumerators' books of 1861 and after was the method by which households were delineated. Double horizontal lines (=) were drawn approximately under the first letter of the name of the last member of a house. Where two households were in the same house, a single horizontal line appears under the name of the last member of the first (-). This system, first used in 1841, replaced the 1851 format of a line drawn across the first four columns to terminate a house entry, and a shorter line to rule off the first household. It allows multiple occupancy to be recognised more easily.

Numerous pencil ticks and crosses appear down various columns of the returns: these were clerical marks made in the process of totalling up the population in various categories. They have no bearing on family history research.

Most researchers start with the most recent available census (1891) having little difficulty in establishing an address at which their family was residing that night. For those who can get no nearer than 1901, the Registrar General, charitably, is willing to waive the hundred year rule of confidentiality in return for £16.75 + £2.93 VAT (the latter is not charged to overseas applicants). The General Register Office at St Catherine's House (*) will release age and place of birth of a specified individual, provided you write for an application form on which you must:

1) provide the precise address where the person was on the night of 31 March 1901.

2) sign a declaration that the information is not required for purposes of litigation, or to be used 'to the detriment of any person'.

Rank, Profession, or Occupation	Where Born	Whether Blind, or Deaf-and-Dumb
	Manchester	
Card Maker	*Jackson Bury*	
do	*Bury Lancashire*	
Card Maker	*do do*	
Coal dealer	*Manchester*	
	Liverpool	
Cabinet turner	*Scotland*	
formerly Employed	*North America British subject*	

Each house is occupied by one household (Ancoats sub-district, Manchester)

31

3) provide the written consent of the person concerned (an optimistic request), or that of his / her direct descendant. Your declaration that you are a grandchild is therefore sufficient.

Drawbacks to this facility are:

1) If the individual wasn't where you expected, you get no refund.

2) The GRO will not inform you even if he were living in the adjacent house.

3) For a search of two addresses you pay double the fee.

Nothing will be released, at present, from later censuses. The 1911 census becomes available in 2012; the 1921 in 2022; the 1931 returns were destroyed by fire; no count was taken in 1941 owing to World War II; and the release dates of returns beyond that are unlikely to trouble any present reader.

Census enumeration was seasonal work, and involved the literate and educated - schoolmasters and overseers of the poor were well represented. Despite an inevitable lack of regular practice, they appear to have done their job with commendable thoroughness, despite low pay. Their reminiscences, lovingly reprinted in various family history society magazines, indicate that the system worked well generally - there was co-operation, once people realised that information would be treated in confidence, and would not reach 'inquisitive

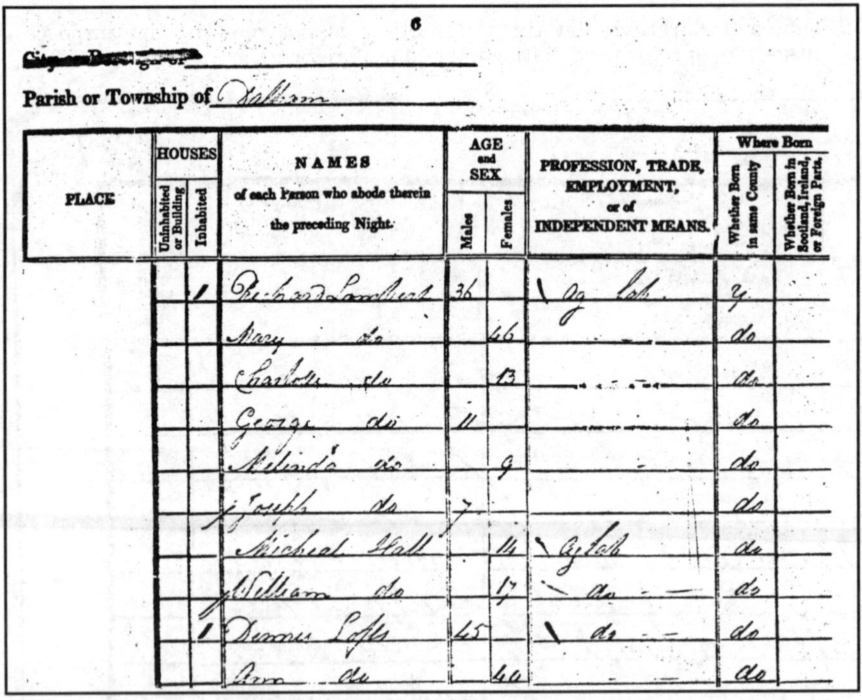

6

~~City or Borough of~~

Parish or Township of Dalham

PLACE	HOUSES: Uninhabited or Building	HOUSES: Inhabited	NAMES of each Person who abode therein the preceding Night	AGE and SEX: Males	AGE and SEX: Females	PROFESSION, TRADE, EMPLOYMENT, or of INDEPENDENT MEANS	Where Born: Whether Born in same County	Where Born: Whether Born in Scotland, Ireland, or Foreign Parts
		1	Richard Lambert	36		Ag Lab	y	
			Mary do		46		do	
			Charlotte do		13		do	
			George do	11			do	
			Melinda do		9		do	
			Joseph do	7			do	
			Michael Hall	14		Ag Lab	do	
			William do	17		do	do	
		1	Dennis Lofts	45		do	do	
			Ann do		40		do	

Figure 13: Top portion of a page of an 1841 enumerator's book - HALLs living with LAMBERTs. Dennis LOFTS is head at the next house (Dalham, Suffolk)

neighbours' (East London, 1901); admittedly, co-operation may have been provided grudgingly by those who 'stood upon their dignity' or suspected that the operation was really designed to uncover income tax liability (Hertfordshire, 1871); and an Eccles enumerator of 1891 reported that 'one man has an only son, John James, aged 5, whose profession is gravely described as "marble player" '. One labourer living in a shed in the farmer's garden recorded his relation to head of household as 'friendly'. To my knowledge, however, obstruction fell short of violence, up to the murder of an enumerator in Northern Ireland in 1981.

EARLIER CENSUSES

Censuses of Great Britain have been taken since 1801. Only population figures exist from the first four (1801-31) not returns, apart from a few odd survivals (eg Great Bolton 1811, 1821 and 1831). These are listed by Gibson (**8**).

Virtually all 1841's returns survive. The government, however, required rather less information from the population than in 1851. Working from left to right in the example in Figure 13, differences were:

1) There were no schedule numbers.

2) Addresses were not specific.

3) Only the first christian name was requested.

4) The clearer system of delineating households (- and =) was used.

5) No relationship to head of family was given.

6) Marital condition wasn't stated.

7) Ages up to 15 were supposed to be exact; above that, they were to be rounded down to the nearest five (hence the frequency of 0s and 5s). Fortunately, many people (including enumerators) couldn't cope with the arithmetical concept involved, and simply recorded the exact age.

8) The question asked with regard to birthplace was 'Are you now living in the county in which you were born?' The answer, yes or no, is not very enlightening. Other possible responses were **I** for Ireland, **S** for Scotland and **F** for Foreign parts. **E** is the equally unrevealing code for any English enumerated in Scotland.

DATES OF CENSUSES

To avoid double counting, people were enumerated at the addresses where they spent the night, or to which they returned after a night's work or travel. It is easiest to refer to individual censuses by the dates on either side of the midnight of census night.

6-7 June 1841	2-3 April 1871
30-31 March 1851	3-4 April 1881
7-8 April 1861	5-6 April 1891

31 March - 1 April 1901

These dates apply to the whole of the UK. They were chosen to minimise distortion of the distribution of the population by seasonal agricultural migration. Relate dates of birth to the above dates when estimating how old a person should be in any particular census year.

ACCESS TO CENSUS RETURNS

There are three places where English and Welsh returns can be viewed:

1) **The Census Rooms of the Public Record Office, Chancery Lane** (*) open six full days a week. 1841-91 are on microfilm; 1891 is also on 'user-friendly' microfiche. In late 1996 they go to the **main PRO site at Kew** (*).

2) **Central libraries** and **county record offices** - most have purchased microfilm of all released census returns for their areas. Gibson (**8**) is a directory of all such local holdings in England and Wales. It details, parish by parish, what each library and record office has for each census year.

3) **Family History Centres of the Mormon Church** - it is possible for members of the public to order individual microfilm reels of any part of the 1841-91 census for the Great Britain (including the Channel Islands, Isle of Man and Scotland) through the Family History Centres. This service currently (1994) costs £2.50 per reel - you then have free use of it at that library for a month, and the period can be extended for a small charge (see also p77). Each centre has a microfiche catalogue, giving a 'call number' for each place in each of the five censuses (ie the reel which needs to be ordered). Towns and cities are cross-referenced under their various districts - you need to have a good idea of which you want, since a town of 100,000 will fill several reels.

OTHER PARTS OF THE BRITISH ISLES

The Channel Islands - returns are in the Census Room of the Public Record Office, Chancery Lane, in London (*), and are also held at the Greffe (*) in the case of Guernsey and the States Public Library, or Societe Jersiaise (*) in the case of Jersey. Note the PRO 1996 change of location, mentioned above.

Ireland - Irish family history research has been uniquely handicapped by the deliberate destruction (by arson) of the Four Courts of Dublin in 1922. Many of the records that are available to researchers in Britain - census returns, wills, parish registers - were wholly or partly destroyed.

A census of the whole of Ireland was taken every ten years, beginning in 1821. The returns from 1861 to 1891 inclusive were never preserved. A portion of the 1821, 1831, 1841, 1851 and the earlier 1813 returns survive for parts of the counties of Antrim, Cavan, Cork, Fermanagh, Galway, King's County (Offaly), Londonderry, Meath and Waterford. Other odd survivals, including a list of 1851 Dublin City heads of household, are described in a useful free leaflet, *Sources for Family History and Genealogy*, available from the National Archives, Dublin (*). All these census returns can be viewed at the National Archives where a detailed list of survivals, *Nineteenth Century Census*, is in the reading room. These survivals can be ordered through Mormon Family History Centres.

The complete 1901 and 1911 returns for the whole of Ireland (modern Eire and Northern Ireland) are available at the National Archives, whilst those for the North for 1901 are also at the Public Record Office of Northern Ireland (*). They are arranged by District Electoral Division, and then subdivided into townlands (the Irish equivalent of an English township, nowadays called a civil parish) or, in urban areas, by streets. In contrast to the English practice, the original returns (those filled in by the heads of household) have not been destroyed - it is these that you see, along with the original returns compiled by the enumerators. Incidentally, they reveal the religion of each person, a question which was to be included in the English census of 1861, unfortunately omitted after opposition.

The 1901 returns can be ordered through Mormon Family History Centres, as can the following three substitutes for the lost Irish censuses:

1) *The Primary Valuation* (also known as *Griffith's Valuation*) was a rating survey carried out between 1847 and 1865. There is a printed valuation book for each poor law union giving the names of all occupiers of land and buildings, together with the extent and value of the holding. These records and an index of surnames arranged by county are also at the National Archives.

2) *Tithe Applotment Books*, compiled between 1823 and 1837, list the occupiers of over one acre of land in each parish, though some urban tenants may be excluded. The surnames index to the Primary Valuation, mentioned above, also covers Tithe Applotment Books. These are at the National Archives (*) or the Public Record Office of Northern Ireland (*).

3) *The Registry of Deeds* in Dublin (*) records most land transactions in the whole of Ireland after 1708 and covers changes of ownership, or of tenancy involving leases for 21 years or more. The original deeds (often containing details from marriage settlements and wills) have been transcribed in full into a series of registers. There is an index of persons granting (ie selling or leasing) the property. The registry is similar to those set up at the same time in England to cover Yorkshire and Middlesex.

The institutions mentioned here will advise whether it is possible to make postal enquiries, or will provide addresses of locally based professional searchers.

The Public Record Office of Northern Ireland (*) holds tithe and valuation records for the province. Also, it has pupil registers for nearly half the 2,000 national public elementary schools of the province, and in about 80% of these cases the registers predate 1900, providing a substitute for the lost 19th Century census returns.

The Ulster Historical Foundation (*), a non-profit making organisation, answers over 1,000 genealogical enquiries a year, provides search assessments free of charge and will undertake professional research in the province.

Isle of Man - census returns with individual names survive only from 1841 onwards, as in England. Microfilm of the 1881 returns is at the Census Room of the Public Record Office, Chancery Lane, in London (*) until late 1996 (see p34); microfilm of 1841-91 is at the Manx Museum Library (*).

Scotland - microfilmed copies of the census enumerators' books of 1841 to 1891 are available for public research at the General Register Office for Scotland (*), immediately outside Waverley Station. There is a daily charge for use of the GRO - see page 76. It is possible to request, by post, a search for a specific person, if you can provide an address. This search costs £5.00.

HOW USEFUL ARE CENSUS RETURNS?

Very. They offer a unique glimpse of individual families, momentarily captured on one day, within the social context of their neighbourhood. Virtually alone amongst British records, they log families rather than individuals. With luck, you may find an immobile ancestral family living half a century in one place. In the space of an afternoon in your library, you can observe them in a succession of census returns. It is hard to bring to mind that the family snapshots you uncover - 1841, 1851 and so on - are moments in time. They tell you nothing of the intervening years of economic slump, ill health, bereavement, day-to-day grind and routine of life in the uncentrally heated and outside-toileted 19th Century.

Census returns recorded parishes/towns of birth in and after 1851, when railway travel was, for the first time, encouraging unprecedented geographical mobility. (You will find that most of the big family moves took place in the railway age of the 1830s onwards.) Returns are a unique bridge between the record-rich Victorian period of birth, marriage and death certificates, and the pre-1837 years when there was no central registration of the population. Without them, you are unlikely to discover the parishes of origin of your ancestors.

They do have limitations. Perhaps 10% of the 'facts' recorded by enumerators were incorrect:

Ages are most suspect. People were not universally convinced that the returns would remain confidential. Agricultural labourers feared that employers, on learning their true ages, might depress wages at the next hiring. Children's ages might be boosted to circumvent restrictions on child labour imposed by the Factory Acts. Teenage girls in domestic service exaggerated their years to secure higher wages. Women married to younger men might prefer not to disclose their true ages, even to their husbands. Over 60s of good character could remain in their own houses on poor relief rather than enter the loathed workhouse.

Relationships to the head of family might be falsified to screen family scandal. An unmarried daughter's illegitimate child was often passed off as the youngest child of the head of household, and not his grandchild. Always subtract the last child's age from his 'mother's', and be suspicious if the difference greatly exceeds 40. Remember that relationships were given to the head of household, and not to his wife. She was not necessarily the mother of all his children.

Places of birth are notoriously unreliable. Around 15% of birthplaces given in urban censuses do not match up with earlier or later census information.

Likely reasons for inconsistency might be:

1) *Ignorance* - my great great grandfather gave four different places of birth in four censuses which reflected the different places he had lived. He forgot his true birthplace because he had lived there so short a time.

2) *Deceit* - any migrant worker thrown out of work faced removal to his parish or township of origin - a sound motive for concealing it, especially since poor law officials often doubled up as registrars and census enumerators. Contrary to common belief, removal did not end with the New Poor Law of 1834 - for example 15,365 people were removed from manufacturing towns in Lancashire, Cheshire and Yorkshire to their places of settlement in the slump years of 1841-3. A Lincoln relieving officer told the 1860 Select Committee on Irremovable Poor that paupers were always removed where a place of legal settlement could be established unless the distance would incur great expense; old people were sent back from the town to their villages to live in 'parish houses'. A Sunderland overseer told the same committee that a woman who had lived there for 35 years was removed to South Shields and would have been sent to Cornwall had that been her legal settlement! Given these prospects, the 1851 census especially must have been seriously affected by the shadow of removal. True, the law gradually fell into abeyance, but local practice varied - Manchester cotton masters who dominated the administration of the local poor law wanted a pool of labour even in slump conditions. More thinly populated and less prosperous poor law unions 15 miles away, however, abandoned removals more slowly.

3) *Generalisation* - the further you are from home. the more likely you are to generalise about your birth place. A man born in Ramsbottom freely admits to the fact in Bury, five miles away; 50 miles from home he generalises and says 'Bury', the nearest large town. In London, he generalises even more, and settles for 'Manchester'. This explanation for false birth places can also be called the 'Where the hell's that?' factor.

This tendency to generalise about birthplaces often makes it impossible to establish any indisputable link with any record of birth solely through census evidence. My great grandfather William LEESON recorded 'Warwickshire, Coventry' on three census schedules (1881-1901) yet the only known birth of anybody of that name at the right time took place some ten miles away, at Knowle. Without other evidence, such as father's name and occupation from William's marriage certificate, this link cannot be forged.

4) *Place names have several meanings* - Halifax was a medium-sized town in Yorkshire in the early 19th Century but was also the location of the mother church of the largest ancient parish in the country, covering hundreds of square miles and many towns and villages. What, therefore, did a 70 year old man mean when he reported 'Halifax' as his birthplace in the 1851 census? A single place name could refer to a village, township, parish or even a manor, each covering a different area.

For both these reasons (**3** and **4**) some knowledge of local historical geography is helpful.

Some other limitations of census returns - in 1891, the head of family had to declare the number of rooms his household occupied, if this were fewer than five, a government attempt to tabulate overcrowding. It is possible that some addresses may be 'light' of children in that year's returns.

Census returns could be less accurate in cases of multiple occupancy, where only one schedule was filled in - a head of household might have made little effort to ascertain details of his lodgers or in-laws.

Human error on the part of the enumerator can't be discounted. It was normal to write the family surname once, and then write 'do' (ditto) each time it was repeated. A grandchild or in-law with a different surname at the end of the schedule could easily be copied mistakenly as a ditto.

The major drawback to using census returns is the fact that they were not compiled for the benefit of family historians - there are no indexes of individuals (although family history societies are now attending to this deficiency, at least in the case of the 1851 and 1881 censuses). If you do not have a precise address at which a family was living at the time of one census, you could face a major search. It can take two hours to search the returns of even a small market town of 5,000 people; and if you know only that your great great grandparents were 'in Birmingham' in 1891 you have real problems ...

FURTHER READING

8 Jeremy Gibson, *Census Returns 1841-1881 on Microfilm* (FFHS, 1990). A new edition, to include the locations of 1891 returns, is (April 1994) expected soon

7 PRACTICAL CENSUS RESEARCH

This chapter deals with some of the difficulties that everybody encounters when using census returns.

FINDING AN ADDRESS IN A CENSUS YEAR

If no index of names has been drawn up, these sources offer some help:

1 LETTERS, FAMILY DOCUMENTS AND ORAL TRADITION Within your, or your relatives' home	**4 BIRTH, MARRIAGE, AND DEATH CERTIFICATES** Your own home, from the district register office or St Catherine's House
2 CEMETERY RECORDS At the cemetery office, town hall or local archives	**5 POST - 1858 NATIONAL INDEXES TO PROBATE RECORDS** District probate registries, record offices or Somerset House
3 TRADE DIRECTORIES, ELECTORAL REGISTERS Larger libraries and record offices	**6 RATE BOOKS** Town hall, library or record office

?

A large town or city, 1891

1) *Letters, family documents and oral tradition* - if you are lucky, one surviving document could pinpoint an ancestral address in 1891, your first target.

2) *Cemetery records* - you will have found in Chapter 5 that cemetery burial registers and graves or order books often contain the precise addresses of their deceased clientele.

3) *Trade directories and electoral registers* - by the late 19th Century, trade directories contain almost complete alphabetical lists of the inhabitants of towns and cities. Electoral registers listed alphabetically, or alphabetically by ward, those eligible to vote (together with their qualifying address) and covered most urban householders after 1867. Even where they are unalphabetical, listing voters in street order, they are still quicker to search than full census returns.

4) *Birth, marriage and death certificates* are worth obtaining in or near census years since all carry addresses - this might only be the name of the town on early ones (many towns had no house numbers until the 1850s). Marriage certificates may provide the same address for bride and groom - these may have been addresses of convenience, to save the cost of having banns read in two parishes, and neither party may have been there on census night. Death certificates may give two bites at the cherry, since the informant (whose address is given, as well as that where death occurred) was almost invariably a close relative.

5) *Post-1858 national probate indexes* invariably provide the full address of city dwelling persons if they left wills, or if their estate was sufficiently valuable for their relatives to require letters of administration. Helpfully, two addresses might be given - the place of death, and the usual abode if this were different. Up to 1 January 1892, addresses of executors or administrators are also entered, together with the relationship to the deceased (executors were commonly their close relatives).

6) *Rate books* (annual lists of those who paid the poor rate) survive from the 18th Century. By the census period, they were large bound volumes listing all the householders of the town or city street by street. The humblest or most transient householders might not have been caught in trade directories, and probably had no vote until 1918. Nevertheless, they would be netted by the overseers of the poor in their annual assessments and collections. Since more than one rate might have been levied in one year, even the most mobile of residents would be included somewhere. In some towns, however, you may find that lodgers and sub-tenants went anonymously as 'and another' after the name of their landlord.

It is far faster to leaf through pages of heads of household in a census year rate book than it is to reel through census returns. (Some libraries have microfilmed these decennial rate books to make them more accessible to researchers.)

PIECE NUMBERS, FOLIO NUMBERS AND PAGE NUMBERS

The enumerators' books were pre-printed and each page pre-numbered - 1, 2, 3 and so on.

The Registrar General stored these completed books in boxes, known as bundles. Depending on its size, one registrar's sub-district might fill one or several of these boxes. When the statutory 100 years had elapsed, the books became public records and were transferred to the Public Record Office. They were microfilmed in strict box order, each frame carrying at its side or base the census year class number (for example RG10 in 1871) followed by the bundle number. So the full bundle reference might be RG10/4008. At the Public Record Office, where English and Welsh returns can be viewed, these bundle numbers are called piece numbers.

During the microfilming process, a new system of pagination was introduced. The first folio (page 1 and its reverse, page 2) in the first book of a bundle was numbered 1, in the top right hand corner of page 1 (see Figure 14). The second folio was numbered 2, and so on, right through that book.

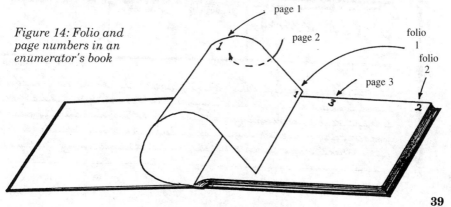

Figure 14: Folio and page numbers in an enumerator's book

This folio numbering continued into the next book to mount up right through the bundle, only beginning again at 1 at the start of the next bundle.

This layout can be found in the enumeration books of 1841 and 1851, although 1841 books were portrait ☐; thereafter they were landscape ☐. In 1861 and later the page numbers were a little off centre, away from the spine. Folio numbers are always bolder than page numbers.

USING CENSUS INDEXES

1) Indexes of individuals

There has been a rapid mushrooming in the number of family history societies since the 1970s. Most have seen the indexing of the 1851 census returns for their areas as an important long term aim. Copies of any indexes are usually in the Census Rooms at the Public Record Office, as well as in the relevant central libraries and county record offices. Many societies are publishing these indexes.

They come in a number of formats so it is vital to read their explanatory introductions. The most ambitious ones index every individual in a sub-district:

Name	Age	Piece No	Folio No
SMITH John	26	568	303

This is a unique reference in the whole of the census. You need only go to the PRO Census Rooms, or to a library where this particular sub-district's returns are available, and ask for the reel on which the piece number is. You can wind through the bundle, watching the folio number steadily increase, until you reach 303. John SMITH should be on the front, or back, of that folio.

Some indexes ignore the uniqueness of the folio number in each bundle, opting instead for enumeration district numbers and page numbers. The enumeration district numbers are to be found on the page entitled *Description of Enumeration District* in the top right hand corner (see Figure 15). They will be a series within each sub-district. Some series run 1, 2, 3; but oddities like 1a, 1b, 1c, 2a and so on may appear, indicating that a parish or township comprises three districts.

Some indexes show only the incidence of surnames within the sub district:

Name	Piece No	Folio Nos
SHANNON	1065	26, 27, 58, 210
	1066	5, 100, 316

Gibson (**10**) lists all census indexes, and their locations, within each county entry. Currently, an ambitious project is in train to index all 26 million people in England and Wales in the 1881 census. County indexes are gradually being published, on microfiche, alphabetically by surname and christian name.

2) Place and Street indexes

Where no index of individuals exists, street indexes are the next best thing, provided you have an address for which to search. The PRO Census Rooms have street indexes, listed in Gibson (**10**), to all towns with over 40,000 inhabitants, indexes to hamlets and specialist street-finding aids for London. Webb (**15**) is also a major help with London census searches.

Most libraries and record offices with holdings of census returns have compiled their own street indexes, some, like Manchester's being on thousands of cards. Often these simply refer you to the number of the enumeration district(s) in which your street lies. They may give the various folios on which the street will appear. These local indexes are sometimes idiosyncratic and it is as well to ask for help from an assistant if you find its rationale beyond you.

A further difficulty is 'the missing street' - small courts and streets may not be in the index, even though you know they existed. It is possible that the indexer missed the name, or couldn't read it. Also, the name may not have been recorded by the original enumerator - he may have included a court with the adjacent street The trick is to ask for a large scale contemporary street map of the area (the 25 inch Ordnance Survey covered urban areas) find your court, and then the name of a nearby large street. This is bound to be in the index. Some trade directories have alphabetical lists of a town's streets, naming in the case of very

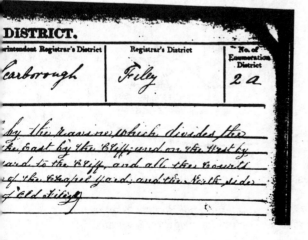

Figure 15: Top portion of the first page of an enumerator's book

small courts or alleys the larger street off which they ran. Street names, and
street numbering, may have changed between censuses.

REGISTRATION DISTRICTS AND SUB-DISTRICTS

The first page of each enumerator's book carries the name of the registration
district (Figure 15, pp40-1). These had been set up, under Superintendent
Registrars, in 1836 to operate the system of civil registration of births, marriages
and deaths which began on 1 July 1837. Each district was coterminous with a
poor law union of parishes or townships.

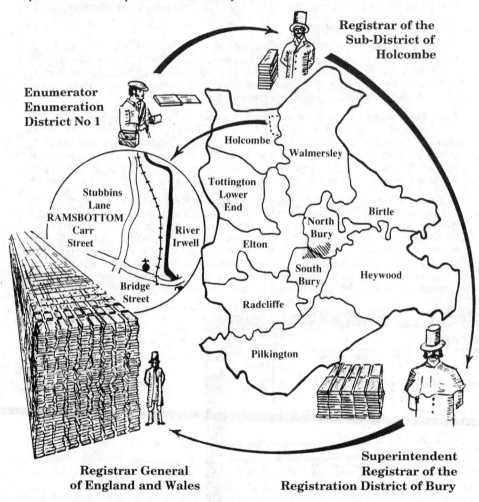

*Figure 16: Taking the census. The enumeration of Ramsbottom, in Bury
registration district, 1851. The actual town of Bury is shaded*

The sub-district is also entered on this first page of the enumerator's book. They too were created in 1836, for the purposes of civil registration, each having a registrar who recorded the births and deaths in his area. The registration district and sub-district appear at the top of birth and death certificates - thus you are led to the correct sub-district of the census returns. Rosier (14) lists all registration districts, county by county (with their PRO piece numbers) for the 1841-91 census returns. For Scotland, see 25, cited on page 77.

The structure of registration districts and sub-districts varied very little before the 1880s and 1890s, and perpetuated old names which had often become archaic. Most sub-districts covered individual parishes or townships and so took names of medieval administrative units. If you are familiar with the Bury area of Lancashire, the sub-districts shown on the map on page 42 will surprise you. Where are the modern towns of Whitefield and Ramsbottom? These were new towns of the 19th Century, and so their census returns must be sought in the sub-districts of Pilkington and Holcombe. Other Lancashire examples are Rochdale (Castleton Within sub-district), Blackpool (Poulton-le-Fylde) and Bacup (Newchurch-in-Rossendale). Similar cases will be found in other 19th Century growth areas and are likely to cause as much confusion to non-natives as 1974 creations like Redbridge, Sandwell and Tameside.

Refer to the *Population Tables* (published within a year or two of each census) to find out in which sub-districts different towns and villages lay. These are available in larger libraries and record offices. Also of interest are the summaries of census returns, published after the 1851 census to provide population figures for each parish and township in the six censuses of 1801-51. They were published by division - Lancashire and Cheshire, for example came under Division VIII, and the full title of their volume was *Census 1851: North*

34 LANCASHIRE.—Parishes. AREA; HOUSES, 1841

No. of District.	No. of Sublist.	DISTRICT or UNION.			Area in Statute Acres.	HOUSES.					
						1841			1851		
		Subdistrict.	No. of Parish.	Parish, Township, or Place.		In-habited	Unin-habited	Build-ing.	In-habited	Unin-habited	Build-ing.
				460 BURY. d							
69	1	Holcombe - -		Bury, part of Parish—* e							
			1	Walmersley-cum-Shuttleworth, part of - - f Township	—	–	–	–	1	–	–
			2	Tottington-Lower-End, part of g Township		954	72	7	1083	56	14
	2	Tottington-Lower-End.		Bury, part of Parish—*							
			1	Tottington-Lower-End, part of g Township	5038	798	102	3	949	58	9

Figure 17: Census Summaries, 1800-51, showing the first two sub-districts of Bury registration district (compare with Figure 16, p42). Unlike these two examples, most sub-districts comprised whole townships or parishes. Reasons for decennial population changes appear as footnotes

Western Counties Numbers of Inhabitants 1801-51. These volumes summarise the reasons provided by overseers and, later, registrars for changes of population in any parish or township, and can be very helpful. For instance, 1821 - 'The increase of population in Over Darwen is partly accounted for by the opening of a new colliery'; in 1841, it was remarked of Fleetwood that 'five years before, the site of the Town was merely a rabbit warren'; and at Newton, in Slaidburn parish, in 1851 the registrar referred to 'agricultural improvements ... on the estate of a proprietor who has brought a considerable number of labourers, partly Irish, into the neighbourhood.' These summaries, like the *Population Tables*, indicate the composition of each sub-district (see Figure 17, p43).

ENUMERATION DISTRICTS AS A UNIT OF SEARCH

It is a fortunate researcher who always has addresses in census years, and always finds his family quickly. Sooner or later, you will have to embark on searches of a whole town, or part of a city to track them down.

Your knowledge of census organisation will make this job easier. When I started, I was reduced to searching by reels for certain elusive Manchester relatives. Pages and pages of entries appeared in my file with arbitrary headings like 'New Cross census, 1851' or 'Ancoats census, 1851', with desperate final notes like 'searched half way through reel 594'. I had little idea of what I had covered on the ground.

First, I needed to keep a record of what areas I'd searched, and I soon decided that searching in units of enumeration districts was the ideal.

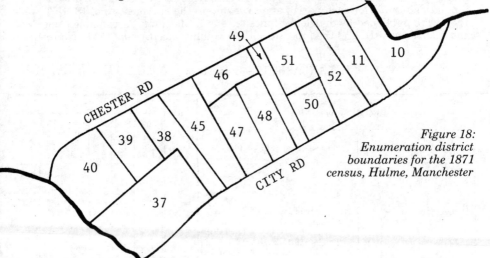

Figure 18: Enumeration district boundaries for the 1871 census, Hulme, Manchester

This portion of the heavily built-up sub-district of Hulme, Manchester shows how some of its enumeration districts were set out in 1871. Main arterial roads mark the two sides of this batch of districts. The other two sides are rivers. The enumeration district boundaries reflect the grid pattern of the streets. Often, they run down the middle of streets, so that even small streets, and not just major ones, can straddle two or more districts.

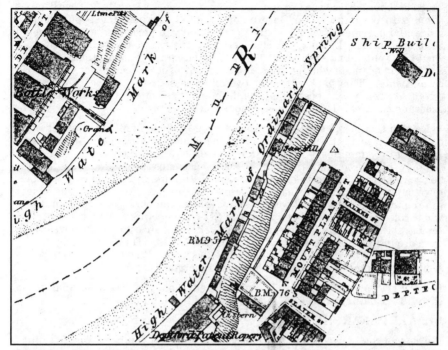

Figure 19: River Wear, Deptford, Sunderland- 25 inch Ordnance Survey, 1857

Enumeration district numbers snake over the sub-district in a baffling manner. If you expected a family to be at an address in ED 38 on our Hulme example and didn't find them, you would assume a short distance move (as most were within 19th Century towns and cities) and want to search adjacent enumeration districts. Unfortunately, maps of the distribution of enumeration districts like this one rarely survive, so it would not be immediately apparent which were the adjoining districts. To follow the direction of the numbering, use a street map in conjunction with the descriptions of each district which appear at the start of each enumerator's book. The Six Inch Ordnance Survey is adequate only to identify the larger streets, but the 25 inch shows every building and names very small thoroughfares. Since people lived very close to their work, such detail also allows likely workplaces to be identified (Figure 19).

Enumeration districts are good units of search for several reasons:

1) You can easily spot the start of a new one by its *Description of Enumeration District* page (Figure 15, pp40-1) - from this you can note down the number as you start searching it. Also, the schedule number starts off afresh at 1 in each new enumeration district. This sheet is followed by the enumerator's statistical summary of his district, and several completed sample sheets.

2) They are manageable - the enumerator had to collect his schedules in one day, so was rarely required to cover more than 500 households. (Only a few city ones spilt over into a second enumerator's book.) Each can therefore be searched in 10 to 20 minutes.

3) Their boundaries were drawn up every ten years to coincide with other administrative units. The Government wanted to know the populations of individual parishes, townships and so on. Ideally, a parish or township would be of such a size that it could be covered by one enumerator. More often, it would be split into two or more districts. You can search all these districts, and then investigate whether there is a collection of other records for your parish or township. This parallel use of two or more sources (a process known as *record linkage*) works best when the different types of record cover the same geographical area. This becomes obvious when you try it.

4) Related families lived close together. If you find one family of relatives in an enumeration district, there is a very strong chance that you will find another. 19th Century families were far more gregarious than today's, and this spirit strongly influenced migration. In my experience, most people moved with, to or before relatives. I used to imagine lone ancestors making a solo trek to a new town or city, but further research has revealed this pattern of family movement in around two thirds of my cases. Many census combers can relate finds of a whole colony of immigrants to a town or city from one particular district. (It is remarkable how many Rossendale researchers have ancestors who moved there from around Cambridgeshire in the 1860s and 1870s.) Towns were frightening places, and the herd instinct provided some security. Rural destinations do not seem to have occasioned so much family magnetism.

Redford (**13**) and Macdonald (**12**) are brilliant, though little used analyses of early 19th Century migration, in England and Scotland respectively.

BLANKET SEARCHES

But do you really need all these relatives? Surely, all you need are your direct lines - forget the rest. Why should it matter that great granddad moved to the same mill town as his brother or cousin? It matters to family history researchers for several reasons:

1) The brother or cousin might have reported his place of birth accurately - great granddad might not.

2) Relatives from an earlier generation might be in the vicinity.

3) The census entries of these nearby relatives may provide crucial clues about family christian name patterns and occupations which are not so obvious in your direct line.

4) Collecting details of families as opposed to individuals gives the wider, truer picture of your origins and is far more satisfying. So, you should take down all instances of an ancestral surname that you find in any enumeration district; and if you have a specific address, do check the whole of the enumeration district for possible relatives. Remember that you may only slot them in as you proceed to other types of records.

Where your surname is just too common in the area, edit the abstraction process by taking out only those families which have:

1) any incidence of an unusual christian name which features in your line.

2) the same, or closely related occupations to those of your line.

3) birthplaces similar to those of your line.

ECCLESIASTICAL DISTRICTS

In urban census returns of 1851 and afterwards, the name of the ecclesiastical district was written in a box at the head of each page (see Figure 12, pp30-1). This will be the name of the Anglican church to whose spiritual care the area had been allocated. It is likely to have been used by many churchgoers in the district and is a clue to where family baptisms, marriages and burials took place.

MISSING FAMILIES

Families were often not where they should have been on census night. Consider:

1) A 'flit' - working class city dwellers were highly mobile. A new workplace or the offer of a cheaper rent could cause them to move house every year or two. Be optimistic - assume short distance moves. Use large scale Ordnance Survey maps to locate potential workplaces - tanneries, stone yards, cotton spinning mills and so on are clearly marked on the 25 inch and larger editions.

2) The workhouse - the lot of the poor (never especially enviable) became even harder after the passage of the 1834 Poor Law Amendment Act for England and Wales. It was never entirely successful in its aim of restricting poor relief to workhouse inmates - in the industrial North it failed completely. But it certainly increased the chances of our humbler ancestors entering these despised 'bastilles'. There were 126,488 people in English and Welsh workhouses on census night in 1851; and the 1841 census, taken during the trade depression of 1837-42, counted 295,856 inmates - one in 50 of the total population.

It follows that ancestors missing from their usual haunts on census night could have been in the workhouse. Each poor law union covered a large area (see the map of Bury union/registration district on p42). There was usually only one workhouse to accommodate paupers from anywhere in the union.

Institutions such as workhouses were treated as separate enumeration districts, and these were always microfilmed at the end of the sub-district in which they lay. The union workhouse was usually near to the main town of the union, although additional parish workhouses from the pre-1834 system sometimes survived to be used for specific categories of pauper - perhaps children.

Workhouse ancestors can often be researched through the institution's records - indoor relief lists, admission and discharge books (often stating where the pauper was going), registers of births and deaths, creed registers (recording names and religious beliefs), and even punishment books - any survivals should be in the local archives, although some may be at the hospitals which now occupy their premises. If you know that an ancestor had the misfortune to suffer a stay in a workhouse, it is worth consulting any surviving minutes of the Board of Guardians' Workhouse Committee to see if his individual circumstances or recalcitrant behaviour justified a mention.

3) Other institutions - your ancestor could have been in prison on census night. This is likely to have been at the county town (Lancaster Castle had 200 reluctant inmates on census night in 1851). Borough jails also existed. Calendars of prisoners, which pinpoint each prisoner's crime and sentence, usually survive amongst Quarter Sessions records at county record offices. A considerable, though less welcome reason for detention may have been lunacy. Colin Rogers points out that around one in 400 were certified lunatics in the late 19th Century. Admission, discharge and case books may throw further light on your ancestor's origins and state of health.

Hospitals, barracks, prisons and asylums, like workhouses, appear in census returns at the end of their sub-district. Since such institutions housed 569,353 people on census night in 1841 (one in 28 of the total population) they should not be overlooked.

4) Specific individuals could be missing from their families for many reasons - there are in the returns of 1841-71 5% fewer under fives than would be expected from civil registration statistics - the youngest child was often forgotten about! (How often do fathers forget, momentarily, that the youngest of a large brood is not to hand?) Canal bargees may have been enumerated anywhere along the stretch of waterway they frequented. One in eight girls and women were in domestic service in 1871, and were some of the most mobile of their sex. (London houses were staffed by women from as far away as Wales and the South West.) Soldiers serving abroad were not enumerated, though seafarers on board ship, in port or at sea, appear from 1851 onwards - see Higgs (11) chapter 7.

5) Other explanations for missing families - the enumerator may have missed their front door. About 1% of all households were omitted from the 1981 census, and in Central London as many as 2.75%. Enumerators' books have gone missing (Woolwich Arsenal and Belgravia, 1861) or have been attacked by damp (parts of south central Manchester, 1851). Pages have been missed during microfilming. Watch for especially short enumeration districts - check the page numbers and population totals at the start of the district. I have found a case where a few pages are supposed to 'include' the returns of several hundred people. In such cases write to the PRO.

RECORDING CENSUS SEARCHES

Pre-printed census forms are useful for census searches. Note down the surname(s) you are looking for, and the numbers of the enumeration districts you have covered. Make a note of those parts which are illegible since rate books might help to overcome the worst difficulties. (The 1841 returns, in pencil, are the worst culprits.) Copy out words that you can't read - you will unravel them later.

Warehouseman   *Domestic*

Copy out all the house, and the details of everybody in the family. This may seem obvious - but I once scribbled down one ancestral lady without her marital condition. This later proved to be a crucial factor in determining what had happened to her husband - so I had to go back and do the work again, properly.

The Census Record Sheet (Figure 20, p49) shows the results of a search for certain names. Always write down the spelling variations you are willing to accept for your surnames. For emphasis, I double underline, in red, directly ancestral families, and single underline collateral ones (ie the families of brothers or sisters of direct ancestors). I leave several lines at the foot of each page for cross references to other sources. Sometimes I find an entry of interest, but outside my search targets. In the example illustrated, Joseph KAY is obviously related to William KAY. I put such entries in square brackets.

Always record boarders, lodgers and visitors. They were often related to the host family. If they were relatives of the wife of the household, they could carry her as yet unknown maiden name. If they were cousins, their names might help to identify the common grandparents.

IS THIS FAMILIAR? THEN YOU NEED ORGANISING!

We offer to the family historian:

★ A4 RECORD SHEETS ★ BOOKS
★ CHARTS/WHEELS/LANCASHIRE MAP
★ POLYPROPYLENE POCKETS
A5/Foolscap/A4/A3/A2
★ POLYPROPYLENE A4/A3 DISPLAY BOOKS

HOW *ALLEN & TODD* STARTED OFF

Like many married couples, we started researching two family trees - record keeping was important because of the geographical diversity of the many lines we were following. We quite simply needed to get ourselves organised!

*Over a period of several years, we tried to solve the problems of record keeping by designing our own standard forms. Gradually, it became apparent that there was a demand from many researchers for a comprehensive system. We listened to suggestions from other researchers to increase the range (**and we still do**). We try to design what people want, and what we know we might use ourselves. One reason we have developed over 60 different record sheets is to cater for as many interests as possible - use what suits you.*

We aimed to keep the price low, so that researchers would not be put off organising their notes on account of expense. We found that elaborate family history record books were costly, and you could only confidently fill them in when you had FINISHED your research - but who ever has?

Our idea is that you simply use the sheets that fit your system. This is why we try to make our range as comprehensive as possible. You can add as many sheets as you want to any part of your file, and then rearrange them if you wish.

We have designed personal details cards if you prefer the index box system. Also our larger pedigree charts and wheels allow you to display ancestry. We believe that ancestors' brothers and sisters and collateral lines are important to successful research, and many of our products allow these, as well as direct lines to be recorded.

.... and no matter how far on you are with your family history, if any of our sheets fit your recording system, you can buy it in packs of 15.

Send for a Comprehensive Catalogue
........*Now!*

STARTER PACKS:

THE EASIEST WAY TO SAMPLE OUR SYSTEM

Our **9 Starter Packs** are an inexpensive means of deciding which of our sheets are of use to you. There are 30 sheets per pack, and each one of our basic range appears in at least one pack.

Choose from the following:

★ *Basic Starter Pack*   ★ *Census*

★ *Civil Registration*   ★ *Parish Register*

★ *Parish & Township Records*

★ *Probate*   ★ *Research Planning*

★ *Scottish Civil Registration*

★ *Reminiscences*

POLYPROPYLENE

ARCHIVE SAFE
PLASTIC POCKETS & DISPLAY BOOKS

Ideal for:-   ★ *charts*
          ★ *photographs*
          ★ *certificates*
          ★ *family documents*
          ★ *photocopies etc.*

ALSO:

A4 & A3 DISPLAY BOOKS

A5/FOOLSCAP /A4/A3/A2 PLASTIC POCKETS

A3 4D-RING BINDERS

HOW TO BUY OUR PRODUCTS:

1. By Post - *Write to us at the address below enclosing a 30p stamp and we will despatch by return a comprehensive catalogue of our products.*

2. By Visiting our Shop in Ramsbottom - *We are situated in the conservation area of the town centre and are one of the most comprehensively stocked family history shops in the country, with many displays of filled-in record sheets and charts. You are welcome to browse for as long as you like in friendly surroundings and will not be under any pressure to buy.*

In addition to **our** *Family History range, we have titles from may other well known Family History and Heritage publishers such as the Federation, Eve McLaughlin and Shire Books, including many titles referred to in Basic Sources. We also stock as large a range of stationery and office essentials as you would expect to find in any large town centre stationery store:*

★ **Computer Stationery**	★ **Files & Binders**
★ **Pens/Highlighters**	★ **Calligraphy Stationery**
★ **Index Boxes/Cards**	★ **Magazine Binders**
★ **Box Files/Wallets**	★ **Good Selection of Paper**
★ **Typesetting Service**	★ **Photocopying** *(certificates reduced to A4)*

★ **Quality Colour Copying While You Wait** *(3 minutes per A4 page)*

Make a day of it!

Visit the attractions Ramsbottom has to offer:

★ **Peel Tower** - *built to commemorate Sir Robert Peel*

★ **East Lancashire Railway** - *Steam trains every hour at weekends and Bank Holidays along the scenic Irwell Valley*

★ **Over a dozen record offices/libraries/archives within a 50 mile radius** - *B & B list available on request*

Record Your Past ...... Let it Survive!

		1851 Census							MANCHESTER (S⁺ GEORGE'S)/ F

Superintendent Registrar's District	**Manchester**		Parish or Township	**Manchester**
Registrar's Sub-District	St George's	Ecclesiastical District	**Christ Church**
P.R.O. Bundle No.	**HO107/2230**	City, Borough, Town, Village	**Manchester**

Record of Search for

D(E)AKIN ; William & Susannah KAY ; SMETHURST/SHETHERS

EDs searched III, Imm (index states these 2 cover all Collyhurst), Inn, Ioo, Ipp, Iqq

Enumeration District No.	Schedule No.	Address	Inhabited House	Name		Relation to Head of Family	Condition	Age of M	F	Rank, Profession or Occupation	Where Born	Deaf-Dumb Blind, Idiot Lunatic
Inn	91	6 James Terrace	I	Edwd DAKIN		Head	M	58		Bookseller	Fairfield	
				Jane	do	Wife	M		59	Annuitant	do	
				Eliz.ʰ	do	Dau			33	Shopkeeper	do	
				Eliza	do	Dau			25	Tea & Tobacco Dealer	Sutton	
Ipp	147	2 Barlow's Buildings	I	George SMETHURST		Head	M	27		Dyer	Lancashire Over Danom Burnley	1
				Elizabeth D.		Wife	M		22		Do Bury	2
				Mary D.		Daur			2		Do Collyhurst	
				Joseph D.		Brother	U	16		Picture Frame Polisher	Do Blackley	
Ipp	172	9 Coates' Buildings	I	William KAY		Head	M	33		Dyer	Lancashire Over Danom	
				Susannah D.		Wife	M		29	Silk Weaver	Do Rhodes	3
				Nancy D.		Daur			4		Do Collyhurst	
				William D.		Son		8m			Do Do	
Ipp	174	25 Coates' Buildings	I	Joseph KAY		Head	M	66		Maker up	Lancashire Over Danom	
				Nancy D.		Wife	M		58		Do Do	
				Robert D.		Son	U	21		Dyer	Do Collyhurst	
				Betty D.		Dau	U		18	Silk Weaver	Do Do	
				Francis D.		Son	U	16		Dyer	Do Do	
				John D.		Son		13		Dyer	Do Do	

1	Bpt. Burnley, 24ᵗʰ Dec 1823, s. Thomas & Mary SMETHERS, Bull & Butcher, Habergham Eaves, Weaver.
2	Bpt. Middleton, 21ˢᵗ Spt 1828, d. John & Hannah DAKIN, Bury, Weaver.
3	Bpt. Blackley, 7ᵗʰ Apr 1822, d Thomas & Mary SMETHURST, Middleton, Weaver.

Figure 20: Census Record Sheet, showing the findings of a search in 1851 census returns (reduced from A4). Space at the bottom is filled with cross references to other sources

49

FAMILY CENSUS RECORD of George SHETHURST

bpt. Burnley S⁺ Peter , 24ᵗʰ Dec 1823, son of Thomas & Mary (SMITH) SMETHURST , Weaver ;
mar. Harpurhey Christ Church, 22ⁿᵈ Nov 1846, Elizabeth DEAKIN, dau of John & Hannah (BOOTH)
D(E)AKIN , Dyer.

1851 Census					P.R.O. Bundle No.	HO 107 / 2230		

Superintendent Registrar's District	Manchester				Parish or Township	Manchester		
Registrar's Sub-District		S⁺ George's			Ecclesiastical District	Christ Church		
Enumeration District No.		1pp			City, Borough, Town, Village	Manchester		
Schedule No. 147		Address 2, Barlow's Buildings, Collyhurst , Manchester						

Name and Surname	Relation to Head of Family	Cond	Age of M	F	Rank, Profession, or Occupation	Where Born		Blind Deaf etc
George SMETHURST	Head	Mar	27		Dyer	Lancashire	Burnley	
Elizabeth Do	Wife	Mar		22		Do	Bury	
Mary Do	Daur			2		Do	Collyhurst	
Joseph Do	Brother	U	16		Picture Frame Polisher	Do	Blackley	

1861 Census					P.R.O. Bundle No.	RG9 / 2964		

Superintendent Registrar's District	Manchester				Parish or Township	Manchester		
Registrar's Sub-District		S⁺ George's			Ecclesiastical District	Christs Church		
Enumeration District No.		38			City, Borough, Town, Village	Manchester		
Schedule No. 93		Address 26, Pickstone S⁺, Harpurhey, Manchester						

Name and Surname	Relation to Head of Family	Cond	Age of M	F	Rank, Profession, or Occupation	Where Born		Blind Deaf etc
George SMETHURST	Head	Mar	38		Cotton Dyer	Collyhurst	Lancashire	
Elizabeth Do	Wife	Mar		33	Silk Picker	Bury	Do	
Mary	Daur	Un		12		Collyhurst	Do	
Elizabeth	Daur	Un		9		Do	Do	
John	Son	Un	4			Do	Do	

1871 Census					P.R.O. Bundle No.	RG10 3996		

Superintendent Registrar's District	Manchester				Parish or Township	Hulme		
Registrar's Sub-District		Hulme			Ecclesiastical District	S⁺ Mark		
Enumeration District No.					City, Borough, Town, Village	Manchester		
Schedule No. 9		Address 21, Medlock S⁺, Hulme , Manchester.						

Name and Surname	Relation to Head of Family	Cond	Age of M	F	Rank, Profession, or Occupation	Where Born		Blind Deaf etc
George SMETHURST	Head	Mar	47		Tripe Dresser	Lanc	Blackley	
Elizabeth Do	Wife	Mar		42		Lanc	Bury	
John Do	Son		14		Works in Cotton Mill	Lanc	Manchester	
William BOWDON	Son-in-law	Mar	26		Grocer's Assistant	Derbysh.	Hayfield	
Mary Do	Daur	Mar		22		Lanc	Manchester	
Benjamin Do	Grandson		4					

Figure 21: Extracts from a Family Census Record Sheet and its reverse - one method of bringing together data from several sources so that patterns and inconsistencies stand out. His 1881 birthplace was Bury! (Reduced from A4)

50

CHECK ALL AVAILABLE RETURNS

It may seem a waste of effort to find your ancestor in all the census years that his/her lifetime spanned, but it is vital for several reasons:

1) Inaccuracy of *where born* column - the Family Census Record on page 50 (Figure 21) shows how one man gave different places of birth in four censuses. Each was a distinct place, and they were up to 20 miles apart. Another ancestor claimed Sunderland in the 1881 census but Birmingham in 1891!

2) Family movement in the early 19th Century - the different places of birth given by adult brothers and sisters, enumerated separately in their own marital homes, may shed light on the movements of their parents in the pre-census period.

3) Discovering previously unsuspected relatives - extended families (usually multi-generational) are believed to have declined during Britain's transition from an agricultural to an industrial economy. In fact, research suggests that the opposite occurred - in Preston in 1851, 41% of widowed, single and separated people over 65 lived with married children, compared with only 26% in surrounding rural areas (see Michael Anderson, *Recent Work on the Analysis of 19th Century Census Returns*, in *Family History*, Vol II, Nos 77-78, (New Series Nos 53/4) August 1980). In one of your returns, another relative may turn up, providing an ancestral birth place going back to the late 18th Century.

4) You need all the information you can get - a sequence of returns may chart intriguing social mobility (from workhouse inmate to prosperous small businessman in one of my cases). Complete changes of occupation may confuse you in other records if you don't pinpoint them from the census returns. Occasionally men regressed in old age to some less skilled or less energetic occupation which figured so early in their lives as to predate the census period. Or, as a trade boomed and declined, men might take it up, and then return to their original occupation in years of slump. This happened amongst my ancestral handloom weavers in Lancashire. Occupations in old age may help to identify the man as a youth.

5) Comprehensive family history - you owe it to your ancestors (and to yourself) to find out all that you can about them.

FURTHER READING

9 Jane Cox, *Never Been Here Before? A First Time Guide for Family Historians at the Public Record Office* (PRO, 1993). £4.95, incl p&p, from the PRO (*)

10 Jeremy Gibson & Elizabeth Hampson, *Marriage, Census and other Indexes for the Family Historian* (FFHS, 1992)

11 Edward Higgs, *Making Sense of the Census* (HMSO, 1989)

12 DF Macdonald, *Scotland's Shifting Population 1770-1850* (Glasgow, 1937)

13 Arthur Redford, *Labour Migration in England 1800-1850* (Manchester University Press, 1976)

14 ME Bryant Rosier, *Index to Census Registration Districts*

15 Cliff Webb, *A Genealogical Gazetteer of Mid-Victorian London* (West Surrey FHS, 1992) - a guide to streets since the 1856 renumbering and renaming

8 TRADE DIRECTORIES, ELECTORAL RECORDS, RATE BOOKS & NEWSPAPERS

The first three are commonly used as means of gaining census addresses, but are also valuable sources in their own right.

TRADE DIRECTORIES

These appeared in quantity in the 19th Century. They were produced to give commercial travellers and potential customers a ready means of locating professional people and tradesmen. Late 18th and very early 19th Century editions can be found, but they tend to list only the handful of more eminent residents. By the late 19th Century, however, directories become very comprehensive, and are virtually alphabetical lists of householders and business proprietors, whether wealthy owner occupiers or working class tenants.

All towns have good runs from about the mid-19th Century, new editions appearing every few years. Small towns and rural areas will be included with the larger towns. County editions were the norm in the less heavily populated parts of the country.

Directories appear in three formats:

1) Alphabetical lists of inhabitants

This 1900 example from Darwen, in Lancashire, illustrates this layout. Lodgers and those in the very humblest accommodation would not be included.

2) Classified lists by trade

> **Ainsworth Edwin, coach-builder, cab proprietor, and funeral undertaker,** Church Bank street and Victoria street ; h. 13 Bank street. Tel. 96
> Ainsworth Mrs. Elizabeth, grocer, 18 Radford street
> Ainsworth Mrs. Ellen, 35 Radford street
> Ainsworth Mrs. Ellen, 10 Marsh terrace
> Ainsworth Henry, fried fish dealer, 25 Duckworth street

Classifications in the these three Darwen examples (1881-1900) run from Agents to Yarn Dealers. Much can be gleaned by abstracting all incidents of your surnames from every available directory. Possible family patterns can emerge - look, for example, at the BURYs and the AINSWORTHs. The health of a family business can be diagnosed (eg William CATLOW). Remember that families often remained occupationally stable for decades or longer. An interesting change here is the likely move of the AINSWORTHs from meat into the allied trade of fish and chip vending. These directories reflect this change in our diet, made possible by the appearance after 1880 of refrigerated holds in fishing vessels.

Butchers.

Ainsworth Hy., 439 Bolton road
Bentley Joseph, 14 Red Earth road
Bury John, 5 Red Earth road
Bury William S., 210 Bolton road
Catlow William, 17 Market street
Chadwick John, 26 Market street

⬆ 1881

⬇ 1891

Butchers.

Barnes John, 3 Hindle street
Bury Edmund, 459 Bolton road
Bury William S., 335 Bolton road
Catlow William, 17 Market street &
  129 Kay street
Chadwick John, 11 Albert buildings

⬇ 1900

Butchers.

Altham Richard, 300 Blackburn road
Bentley Hargreaves, 45 Kay street
Bury Elizabeth J., 335 Bolton road
Catlow William, 6a and 17 Market
  street, Kay street, and Olive lane
Chadwick John, 9 and 11 Albert bldgs

3) Lists of inhabitants street by street

Late 19th Century editions may have sections like this Ramsbottom example of 1888, though usually with an alphabetical and/or classified portion too. Like rate books, they allow you to scan large areas very quickly, and are an excellent gauge of the tone of your ancestor's neighbourhood.

ANNIE STREET, *Regent Street.*	BOLTON ROAD NORTH, *Stubbins.*
2 Timms John, mason	(Left hand side.)
4 Houlker James, block printer	Briggs John, chapel keeper
6 Atherton John, labourer	STUBBINS BOARD SCHOOLS
8 Campbell James, labourer	151 Parkinson Thos. pattern designer
10 Woolley Josiah, policeman	153 Nocher Duncan, printer
12 Longworth Sarah, householder	155 Farrar Joseph, carter
14 Bridge William. weaver	157 Barker Lambert, tenter

Some 18th and early 19th Century directories were often published by public subscription and may exclude those who didn't want the publicity. They all took time to compile, and so reflect the situation in the town months or perhaps a year or more earlier. Also, some unscrupulous publishers used old editions for their lists. Hence, entries may become fossilised.

Other information in directories

Directories generally are evocative memorials of the detail of 19th Century life with their advertisements, mail coach departures, 'last post' times, names and addresses of the district overseers of the poor and the like. More substantially for family historians, the entries for each town are usually prefaced with an historical introduction. These often provide details about:

a) local trades (and often, usefully, when they and perhaps therefore their workers came to the town).

b) local canals and railways, again with dates - valuable clues to migration patterns.

c) churches and chapels, normally with dates of foundation, and in the case of older Anglican churches the year when the parish registers began.

d) municipal cemeteries, including opening dates.

e) local government - helpful when you pursue other classes of records since you need to know the parish, township, borough or manor under whose jurisdiction your families lived.

ELECTORAL RECORDS

The franchise before 1832

There have been two types of election in Britain - for parliament and for local government.

The basic voting qualification before 1832 was the ownership of freehold land (as opposed to the leasing of land) worth 40 shillings (£2) a year. This was a theoretical valuation, like modern rateable values - it meant that the property was estimated to be worth £2 a year to the owner if he rented it out.

Prior to the Reform Act of 1832, the voting qualifications were:

Franchise	Parliamentary Elections	Local Elections
Boroughs	Boroughs always elected their own MP(s) - the qualification varied from borough to borough	Boroughs had *corporations* elected by some or all of the borough's *freemen*, on the same franchise as in parliamentary elections
Counties outside boroughs	Counties outside boroughs were always represented separately. The *county franchise* was based on the ownership of freehold land assessed as worth 40 shillings or more a year to its owner	Apart from poor law union boards of guardians, there were no elected local councils outside boroughs until the formation of county councils in 1888. Prior to that, local government was in the hands of manor, parish or township officers, and above them the county magistrates

In 1831, on the eve of the Reform Act, about 478,000 men (out of a population aged 21 or over in England and Wales of ten million) had any say in the choice of their MP - perhaps 10%. It took 96 years to achieve adult suffrage (see Figure 22).

Types of electoral records

1) POLL BOOKS were a record of everybody who had actually voted in a disputed (ie contested) election. Most are post 1711. The 1807 poll book for Yorkshire is typical. It lists 25,000 voters, alphabetically in township, which are themselves arranged alphabetically. It gives their occupations, for whom they voted, and (of crucial value) the township in which their qualifying freehold property lay. In numerous cases, this was not their township of residence. Thus you have an indication of where they had property (and therefore possibly family) contacts. At the end of the volume are the *Foreign Voters*, those not resident in the county, but who owned sufficient Yorkshire freehold to make them voters there. Most usefully, the township where this lay is named. Thus, in Bolton, Lancashire, we find:

BINKS	George	Grocer	freehold in Hawes
BINKS	John	Carpenter	freehold in Hawes

- clear indication of likely family origins, over 40 years before any census return provides place of birth. 42 Manchester residents, and around 300 Lancashire residents in all, owned Yorkshire freehold. Poll books are therefore invaluable sources for cross-county and inter-county movement in the 18th and early 19th Centuries. Many were printed after the elections in question and several copies for each election year may survive for each county. See Gibson (**17**) for locations.

2) LAND TAX RETURNS were, between 1780 and 1832, effectively the county electoral register, since payment of this tax qualified men over 21 to vote outside the boroughs. These returns are arranged by parish or township, and list everybody paying Land Tax. They form part of the Quarter Sessions records at county record offices.

3) BURGESS or FREEMEN'S ROLLS were not electoral registers in the modern sense since in many boroughs the ruling body was a self perpetuating elite. They

	Boroughs	Counties outside boroughs	Comments
1832	The traditional franchise of each borough continued, with the addition of householders (ie occupier, whether owner or tenant) of property assessed as worth £10 a year	Freeholders with property worth 40s a year. Copyholders renting property at £10 a year. £10 leaseholders with at least 60 years leases. £50 leaseholders with at least 20 years leases. Any tenant paying more than £50 a year	By 1833, c814,000 voters - richer industrialists, merchants and substantial farmers Voters - 1 man in 7
1867	Every adult male householder resident for a year and heads of families lodging in unfurnished rooms paying £10 a year in rent	Any owner or leaseholder of property rated at £5 a year, or tenant of property rated at £12 a year	1,430,000 in 1866 2,500,000 in 1868 This now included most working men in towns and cities but excluded rural labourers
1869	Some women received a vote in local elections		Voters - 1 man in 3
1884	No change	Same voting qualifications as granted to the boroughs in 1867	3,200,000 in 1883 5,900,000 in 1885 Most rural labourers now received the vote but still excluded were heads of households who shared houses; adult males living with parents(s); soldiers in barracks; and women Voters - 2 men in 3
1918	All males over 21 (residents or owners); women over 30 who were householders or wives of householders - 6 women in 10 Plural voting was limited to one residential and one business or university qualification (previously a man could vote in any constituency where he met the property qualification)		Voters - 5 people in 6 over 21
1928	Every resident or owner over 21		97% of the adult population
1948	Abolition of business/non-resident ownership vote and university seats		
1969	Everybody over 18		

Figure 22: The growth of the franchise

were lists of freemen of the borough, (ie those permitted to trade within the town or city) although in some boroughs the freemen were all voters. Qualification as a freeman varied but was usually achieved by inheriting the right, by completing an apprenticeship in the borough or by purchase. Two Lancashire examples will illustrate the wealth of these records:

The Rolls of the Freemen of Lancaster 1688-1840 (printed by the Record Society of Lancashire & Cheshire, Vol 90) are an alphabetical list of those entitled to vote, and indicate a recurrent theme in electoral records - the right to vote in a place far away from where you were actually living. For example, admitted to freedom of the borough in 1806/7 was James MOISER, of Liverpool, wheelwright, son of John MOISER of Skerton, yeoman. Other entries (some giving ages) indicate similar family moves away from Lancaster.

The Rolls of the Burgesses at the Guilds Merchant of Preston 1397-1682 (Record Society of Lancashire & Cheshire, Vol 9) are especially useful in constructing pedigrees. Later rolls are still at Preston Town Hall. Sons of freemen could be sworn at 21, irrespective of where they lived. Preston was the most democratic town in Lancashire - males over 21 could vote in borough elections after 1768.

A list of pre-1835 English and Welsh boroughs is most readily available in Richardson (**21**) and West (**23**).

Some of these boroughs experienced decline and had ceased to enroll freemen long before the 19th Century.

4) REGISTERS OF ELECTORS have been compiled annually since 1832. Borough registers perpetuated the archaic names of *burgess rolls* or *citizens' rolls*. Earlier ones are alphabetical, or at least all surnames are grouped by initial letter. Late 19th Century registers are often alphabetical by ward (or by the smaller polling districts) and this has made the 1891 census more accessible than its predecessors, since the 1884 Act enfranchised virtually every male head of household.

The property qualification can lead to interesting cross references, as in this 1885/6 Manchester example:

Benjamin GRAY; **abode** - Westcombe Lodge, Wimbledon, Surrey;
qualification - freehold warehouse; **description** - 10 Pollard St, Gt Ancoats St

In very large cities registers can be useful in tracing the places of abode of city centre shopkeepers and tradesmen since both addresses are given.

Look out for separate sections for *Ownership Voters, Occupiers Lists* and *Lodgers List* and even an appendix of those put on the register late. Especially useful for tracing World War I servicemen and their units are the *Absent Voters' Lists* (for 1918 and 1919 only) which give, for each absent voter, 'Description of Service. Ship, Regiment, Number, Rank, Rating . . . or recorded address'.

Regrettably, electoral registers deteriorate in usefulness, eventually becoming simply a list of householders in each street. Nevertheless, where a family remains at one address for two or more generations, a change of name may be a clue to a man's death, and his widow or son becoming the householder. After 1918, several adults in a household might have the vote. So the registers become annual censuses of adult residents at each address - a source for tackling cases of dubious paternity in cases of illegitimacy.

They also allow the inexpensive pursuit of 20th Century collateral descendants of earlier ancestors. Between 1918 and 1971 the year in which a person's name enters the register at their parent's address is a clue to age (see Figure 22, p55). The precise day on which a person becomes an elector (their 18th birthday) appears from 1971 onwards. Birth entries in the National Indexes at the GRO provide the mother's maiden name starting in 1911 (see p68) - a marriage index search will confirm the parents' christian names and provide the year and district of marriage. A man's year of death can be deduced when his widow begins to appear alone - this can lead to a will (see pp79 and 83).

Unfortunately, electoral registers can mislead. From 1867 to 1918, there was a year's residence qualification, and a six month gap between the compilation of a register and its coming into force. An elector could have moved into an address months before he appeared in any register.

Even today, local authorities may continue to include electors who submit no return, they having died or moved away years before.

Look for electoral registers in record offices, central libraries and town halls. (Unfortunately, they got so large after 1884 that their bulk has made them vulnerable. Lancashire Record Office, for instance, keeps only one year in five after 1881 and destroys the remainder.) The Census Rooms at the Public Record Office, Chancery Lane (*) have a set of English and Welsh electoral registers dating from the 1870s - book an appointment to see them via the Enquiry Desk.

RATE BOOKS

The modern British rating system grew out of the obligation of parishes and townships to support their own poor. The overseers of the poor levied a rate on the houses and land of the parish. They needed to keep a record of each person's assessment and whether or not it had been paid. Such rate books may survive from the 18th Century. They are effectively annual lists of all householders of the parish, and often name the farm or property for which rates were paid. Comparisons between different years or months can throw up evidence of decease and continued occupation by the widow or heir (see Figure 23). Even if no addresses are given, a good deal can be learned by studying groups of properties over several years.

				John Marsden			
Jno Bailey John Strickland		3-0		John Bayley ~~Widow Strickland~~		2-0	
George Taylor		2-3		George Taylor		1-6	
for Smithy		1-0		for Smithy		8	3-6
Do John Fletcher		1-3	5-3	Do John Fletcher		10	
James Howarth		0-9		James Howarth		6	
John Barlow		1-9	3-6	Excrs of Jno Barlow John Allen 1-2		2-4	
Do John Booth		1-9		Do Geoe Booth		1-2	

Figure 23: Rate book extracts for the township of Pilkington, Lancashire, 1800, the sums payable being in shillings and pence. Left - January ; right - April

Many householders remained in situ from one assessment to the next, and so act as fixed points from which to identify changes of occupant in other houses. Note the evidence in Figure 23 of sub-letting by George TAYLOR and John BARLOW, and some multiple occupancy.

57

Where house order in the list changes, however, properties can still be identified from the rates paid on them. Rateable value was a constant from year to year, and so the sums assessed for two properties would always be in the same ratio.

Those exonerated from payment, on the grounds of poverty, may be indicated.

By the census period, most towns have long runs of annual rate books. This helps to throw up information which does not appear in the decennial census returns. One of my 'problem' families went into Blackley workhouse, near Manchester, in the 1830s, the father Thomas SMETHURST having disappeared from known records, and therefore presumed dead or absconded. In 1842, his wife, Mary SMETHURST, appeared in the rate book for the adjacent township of Harpurhey, on Pleasant Street (houses were not numbered). She died in 1843. The following year, Thomas appeared as a ratepayer on the same street, sharing a house with someone who was (judging by the surname) a relative of his mother. Apparently a marital breakdown had occurred (Mary had had an illegitimate son in 1835) but Thomas returned to his children when his wife was out of the way. In the 1851 census, there was no trace of Thomas anywhere in the area. Without the yearly rate books, none of this could have come to light.

No	No of House	Name of Occupier	Name of Owner	Description of Property rated	Rent per week	Gross Estimated Rental	Rateable Value	PoorRate at 6s 8d in £
3109	16 Upper Cyrus St	Wm Leeson	Geo. Percival	House	4/6	£8 15s	£7 5s	£2 8s 4d

1st rec. Sept 28th £1 18s 8d

Figure 24: The entry for a single dwelling in a Manchester rate book, 1901

Late 19th Century rate books are detailed. Figure 24 is an entry from a giant 1901 volume for Bradford, Manchester. The immense mass of these records means that some town halls could fill rooms with their growing collections. Consequently, some town have become victim to the shredder, notably during the World War II National Salvage Campaign. Liverpool's complete collection was destroyed in the 1930s, but many authorities have fortunately taken a more enlightened view, and have deposited them in the central library or record office.

RETURNS OF OWNERS OF LAND, 1873-6

Parliamentary concern that land ownership had become unhealthily concentrated led to the compilation in 1872-3 of alphabetical lists, by county, of the 972,836 owners or 99 year lessors in England and Wales (outside London) of an acre or more (HMSO, 1875). Thus John James COOPER of Rainow, Cheshire held 27 acres at a rental of around £40. The equivalent *Return of Owners and Heritages in Scotland 1872-3* (HMSO, 1874) includes about 240,000 names. The return for Ireland (1876) often gives precise addresses in Great Britain or Dublin for the many non-resident owners (Parliamentary Papers,1876, volume LXXX). These returns can be seen in many large libraries (those for England and Wales are also in the Census Rooms of the PRO) and most counties' returns can be purchased on microfiche (at between £1.50 and £3.50) from Rosemary Cleaver, 17 Lane End Drive, Knaphill, Woking, Surrey GU21 2QQ).

LOCAL NEWSPAPERS

You need only glance at the contents of a modern local newspaper to appreciate how fruitful they will be for future family historians. In the last century, even relatively small towns had their own weekly newspaper, and local life was generally far less eventful - so journalists reported minutiae in even greater detail than that which clogs the modern local press.

Some local papers date back to the 18th Century, but most start in the 19th. They contain a vast store of family history information - but it is a largely untapped one since most newspaper runs are unindexed.

Three locations might house back issues or, more likely, microfilm copies:

1) The offices of the newspaper, or its successor.

2) The local authority's central library (which could be miles away from the town in which the paper was published) or the county record office.

3) The British Newspaper Library (*) - opposite Colindale tube station, on the Northern Line, is open six days a week, from 10-00am to 4-45pm, and is heavily used. It holds 20 miles of shelving of English, Welsh, Scottish and Irish newspapers, the runs of which are very comprehensive from 1840 onwards. English and Welsh coverage is particularly good, and nearly half the Scottish titles are represented. There is a catalogue. There are 36 microfilm readers and you can use typewriters and portable tape recorders. Visitors need identification.

Photocopies of items can be ordered by post, as long as you can supply accurately dated references, so pick up a wad of order forms if you do make a visit. Send for several copies at once, since the minimum charge by post is £11.75. The Library will supply a list of professional research workers who are willing to work there.

Gibson (**16**) contains the dates, and usually the locations, of all known titles. Long runs can survive in private hands. Local knowledge is useful in locating back copies.

There are some avenues into local newspapers:

1) Many libraries have drawn up indexes of subjects and individuals, especially obituaries, although only the more eminent will have been honoured with one.

2) Death certificates indicating decease in violent or suspicious circumstances normally lead to contemporary newspaper coverage of the event, which may reward the researcher with lurid details reported from an inquest. A friend of mine discovered from a death certificate that an ancestor was killed in an explosion in his own bakery. The newspaper report carried details of the man's death, but also about his business activity and much more previously unknown biographical information almost certainly recorded nowhere else. For our period, newspapers are likely to be the best source for inquests. See Gibson & Rogers (**18**).

3) Incidents involving an ancestor are often remembered because of a vague connection with a national figure or event. These can usually be dated

accurately from standard reference works such as the *Dictionary of National Biography. British and Irish Biographies 1840-1940* (Chadwyck-Healey Ltd, 1990) indexes, on fiche, over half a million biographical pieces in138 journals.

4) Local tradesmen often commissioned regular advertisements - valuable insight into the scope of their business.

5) Where several ancestral families are known to have lived in a community, a patient trawl may be worthwhile. Local newspapers came out weekly; and it is easy to master their format - advertisements on the front page, national news (copied from daily nationals) on pages two to three, items from the various districts of the locality featured on other specific and time honoured pages - in these circumstances, it doesn't take too long to scan a full year, provided you are not enmeshed by saucy detail.

There are some especially rewarding items to be found:

1) Births, Marriages and Deaths - such an event many miles away from home territory could be featured.

2) Funerals and weddings were scrupulously reported if the parties belonged to the respectable classes - a lengthy inventory of mourners (with relationships to the deceased) could be invaluable.

3) Reports of prosecutions for offences ranging from drunk and disorderly to 'furiously riding a bicycle' can shed completely new light on the character of your ancestors. (In the course of research in the *Filey Post*, my wife and I came across a particularly depressing case of child neglect - my wife has a very distant cousin in Scarborough whom we know well - we haven't the heart to tell him that it was his grandfather who was convicted of this offence in the 1890s.)

4) Finally, some real gems can be found:

a) As early as the 1780s, the *Manchester Mercury* has lists of fathers of illegitimate children (with abodes and occupations) who had failed to answer recognisances, together with the names of their female partners.

b) Lists of oldest inhabitants, with ages, appear in reports of special church parties held for their benefit.

RELATIVES IN THE SERVICES

There were 5,000,000 Britons in uniform during First World War, so its participants are likely to be encountered in every family - electoral registers, newspaper cuttings, surviving medals or family tradition are the clues. Deaths in World War I can be dated from *Soldiers Died in the Great War* (HMSO,1920) a series of booklets contained in many larger libraries which detail the full name, place of birth and enlistment (with place of residence if different to the latter), army number, rank and date of death of some 667,000 soldiers killed whilst serving in a British unit. *Officers Died in the Great War* details the 37,000 officer deaths. Both were republished in 1988 by the Imperial War Museum.

The Commonwealth War Graves Commission (*) has details of all the Commonwealth's military dead from the two world wars - 1,114,804 in the First (80% British), and 580,085 in the Second (66% British). This information is contained in registers of cemeteries or of memorials. Since the Commission has card indexes to all these 1,694,889 servicemen, it should be able to provide (free to relatives, otherwise £1 per trace) the location of the soldier's grave, and information from the cemetery register which will give his age, and the name and address of his next of kin. It can also arrange for a photograph of the grave to be taken, at a charge of £6.25. The Commission can furnish similar detail about the rather fewer Royal Navy deaths. See Wilson (**24**) for RAF personnel. Follow up the date of *any* military death in the local newspaper. There may be a short piece, and perhaps even a photograph of the deceased.

About half the entries in the Commission's registers contain personal information supplied by the family. Registers can be bought for £3.50, a fascinating way of seeing the context of comrades with whom your relative died, just as the dates in *Soldiers Died* hint at the actions in which his unit fought.

Details of the service record of a Great War soldier may survive at the Ministry of Defence (*) and will be released on receipt of written consent from the next of kin. First World War medal entitlement can be ascertained from the MoD's alphabetical card index, now on microfiche in the Microfilm Reading Room at the PRO, Kew (*). It provides surname, first christian name and any other initial, regiments in which the man served, service number and medals issued. Since every soldier who served in a war theatre received the British War Medal, this index is the simplest means of identifying Great War soldiers, regardless of whether they survived or died (see PRO Information Sheet 101).

It is also worth obtaining a photocopy of the entries in the unit's War Diary for the day of the soldier's death - available from the Public Record Office, Kew (*) - class no W095. This might contain a vivid report of the circumstances in which he was killed, even though it is very unlikely that ordinary ranks will be personally named.

A census entry 'Chelsea pensioner' may be your first clue to an earlier military ancestor. From 1873 to 1913, there are at the Public Record Office, Kew (*) alphabetical indexes to class WO97 - discharge papers. Only those who died in service will be omitted. The papers will give full details of the soldier's military career, place of birth and age at enlistment. See Watts (**22**).

FURTHER READING

16 Jeremy Gibson, *Local Newspapers 1750-1920 England & Wales; Channel Islands; Isle of Man: A Select Location List* (FFHS, 1991)

17 Jeremy Gibson, *Poll Books c1695-1872* (FFHS, 1990)

18 Jeremy Gibson & Colin Rogers, *Coroners' Records in England & Wales* (FFHS, 1992)

19 Norman Holding, *World War One Ancestry* (FFHS, 1991)

20 NAM Rodger, *Naval Records for Genealogists* (HMSO, 1988)

21 John Richardson, *Local Historian's Encyclopedia* (Historical Publications, 1986)

22 CT & MJ Watts, *My Ancestor was in the British Army: How can I find out more about him?* (SoG, 1992)

23 John West, *Town Records* (Phillimore, 1983)

24 Eunice Wilson, *The Records of the Royal Air Force. How to find the Few* (FFHS, 1991)

9 CIVIL REGISTRATION OF BIRTHS, MARRIAGES AND DEATHS

ENGLAND AND WALES

The English government relied on the church to register the population from 1538 to 1837. Unfortunately, the system was never comprehensive and no single central register existed. Government concern over education, health and child labour prompted the introduction of a civil system from 1 July 1837. Parish registration continued, however, providing a parallel system which can still be of great use to family historians, as long as they know the church that their family has used.

Registers of births and deaths have been kept by the district registrars since that date, although the Church of England continued to be entrusted with the registration of marriages. Register office marriages began at the same time, but accounted initially for a very small fraction of the total, usually involving those who had little liking for the Anglican church. (Another innovation of 1837, often used by nonconformists, was marriage by superintendent registrar's certificate. These were issued after three weekly readings of the marriage notice at board of Guardians' meetings, whose minutes may record length of residence.)

Copies of these local registers were sent quarterly to the General Register Office. Very careful checks have always been made on these copies as they arrive, so that an almost perfect parallel set of the local entries is accumulating in London.

CERTIFIED COPY OF AN ENTRY OF DEATH   Given at the GENERAL RE

Applicatio

REGISTRATION DISTRICT	*Leigh*					

1840. DEATH in the Sub-district of *Atherton & Tyldesley* in the *County of*

No.	When and where died	Name and surname	Sex	Age	Occupation	Cause of death	Signature, description, a: residence of informant
Columns :— 1		2	3	4	5	6	7
171	*Thirtieth of May 1840 at Tyldesley*	*Robert Lord*	*Male*	*79 years*	*Shoemaker*	*Dropsy*	*The mark of x James Lord present at death Tyldesley*

CERTIFIED to be a true copy of an entry in the certified copy of a Register of Deaths in the District above mentioned.
Given at the GENERAL REGISTER OFFICE, LONDON, under the Seal of the said Office, the   *20th* day of *February* 198*0*

DA 714049

This certificate is issued in pursuance of the Births and Deaths Registration Act 1953. Section 34 provides that any certified copy of an entry purporting to be sealed or stamped with the seal of the General Register Office shall be received as evidence of th or death to which it relates without any further or other proof of the entry, and no certified copy purporting to have been given in the said Office shall be of any force unless it is sealed or stamped as aforesaid.
CAUTION:— Any person who (1) falsifies any of the particulars on this certificate, or (2) uses a falsified certificate as true, knowing it to be false, is liable to prosecution.

Figure 25: Certified copy (made in 1980) of an entry of death - i

The locally held registers and the London copies are not open to public inspection (although this situation may soon change). You can only obtain information from them in the form of a certified copy, which the state guarantees (rather ambitiously) to be a true copy of an entry in its registers. These cost £5.50 each.

FORMAT OF CERTIFICATES IN ENGLAND AND WALES

Death Certificates 1837-1969

These carry the least genealogical information. The ages are always suspect - in the case shown below, who, in 1840, would have been alive in 1761 and therefore have first hand information of Robert's birth? Beware of *age heaping* - numbers ending in 0 and 5 are especially likely to be guesses, but 2 and 8 also figure disproportionately often, when people report ages.

Informants were almost invariably relatives, though the relationship was unspecified in the earlier years of the system - women with surnames different to the deceased were probably married daughters. Up to 1874, causes of death were usually furnished by the informant. These Manchester diagnoses indicate the lack of medical polish of the period:

'Decline' (57 years)	'Fever' (very common)
'Dentition' (17 months)	'Tooth Fever' (11 months)
'Worms' (4 years)	'Water in Head', (2 years)
'Blow with Poker' (63 years)	'Turn of Life' (50 years)

Violent deaths should always be pursued in the local newspaper, where coroners' inquests were often reported verbatim.

Robert LORD's death certificate (Figure 25) issued in 1980, was a copy of a copy of the original entry made by Thomas SALE, the Atherton Registrar, in 1840. Copy one was made for the quarterly return to London in 1840; copy two was made from copy one in 1980.

The GRO at St Catherine's House has recognised the risks of error in copying. Most issued there now carry a photocopy of the copy originally received from the local registrar. The birth certificate (Figure 26) is an example.

Birth Certificates 1837-1969

Births could be registered within six weeks at no charge; thereafter it cost 7s 6d, a powerful incentive for informants to state that a birth had occurred later than it did. This explains why some people find they have two birthdays - a true one, and an 'official' one.

Where a time of birth was given, this implies twins or more, though from 1837-9 some conscientious registrars recorded the time of birth as a matter of course. This practice persisted longer in some districts, and was especially common in the Scottish system.

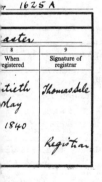

R OFFICE, LONDON.

r 1625 A

aster

8	9
When registered	Signature of registrar
tieth May 1840	*Thomas Sale* *Registrar*

eath certificate'

1888. BIRTH in the Sub-district of *Ancoats Manchester* in the *County of Lancaster*

REGISTRATION DISTRICT *Manchester*

Columns:— 1	2	3	4	5	6	7	8	9	10*
No.	When and where born	Name, if any	Sex	Name and surname of father	Name, surname and maiden surname of mother	Occupation of father	Signature, description and residence of informant	When registered	Signature of registrar	Name entered after registration
182	*Sixteenth September 1888 52 Sandal Street*	*Margaret Grice*		*William Leeson*	*Isabella Leeson formerly Robson*	*General Labourer*	*I. Leeson Mother 52 Sandal Street*	*Twenty ninth October 1888*	*E Watkin Registrar*	✓

CERTIFIED to be a true copy of an entry in the certified copy of a Register of Births in the District above mentioned. Given at the GENERAL REGISTER OFFICE, LONDON, under the Seal of the said Office, the *30 th* day of *March* 19*78*

*See note over

BXA 353536

This certificate is issued in pursuance of the Births and Deaths Registration Act 1953. Section 34 provides that any certified copy of an entry purporting to be sealed or stamped with the seal of the General Register Office shall be received as evidence of the birth or death to which it relates without any further or other proof of the entry, and no certified copy purporting to have been given in the said Office shall be of any force or effect unless it is sealed or stamped as aforesaid.

CAUTION:—Any person who (1) falsifies any of the particulars on this certificate, or (2) uses a falsified certificate as true, knowing it to be false, is liable to prosecution.

Form A502M S.365777 Dd 412987 65M 7/77 Hw.

Figure 26: Certified copy of an entry of birth, containing a photocopy of the quarterly return sent to the GRO in 1889

Illegitimacy is implied by omission of the father's name, although some unmarried mothers did register this piece of information. After 1875 some protection was afforded to the hapless man - he had to be present to consent to his name being entered.

Marriage Certificates 1837-present

Ages are very suspect for clear reasons and many mid-19th Century certificates give only the limited information shown in Figure 27. Be suspicious of any claim that bride and groom lived at the same address. This was a ploy to avoid the trouble of having banns called in two parishes. As in the case of ages, it was far easier to conceal the truth in urban rather than rural parishes, where the couple would probably be personally known to the clergyman and his clerk.

Again, a blank in the father's column indicates uncertainty about his identity, a likely sign of illegitimacy.

A father might be described as 'deceased', but absence of this information does not necessarily mean that he was alive at the time of the wedding.

Witnesses were usually relatives - it was also common for

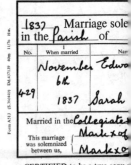

CERTIFIED COPY OF AN

1837 Marriage sole in the *Parish* of

No.	When married	Nam
429	*November 6th 1837*	*Edwa* *Sarah*

Married in the *Collegiate* This marriage was solemnized between us, { *Mark x of* *Mark x o*

CERTIFIED to be a true copy

Given at the GENERAL REGISTE

This cer be sealed or st and no certified

MB 187812

CAUTION:—

There a

a courting couple to act in this capacity. Where a wedding party could not furnish a couple of literate guests, the parish clerk usually offered his services, although this will not be apparent from a single certificate - you would need to see a sequence of marriages in the register to spot one signature appearing regularly.

Death Certificates 1969-present

The GRO came to the remarkable conclusion that informants registering a person's death were more likely to report dates of birth accurately than ages! Consequently, this information was required after 1 April 1969. My grandmother's date of brth was wrongly reported by her son as 26 September 1888 at her death in 1974 - compare with her birth certificate (Figure 26). My other grandmother also fouled up the new system - my father registered her death in 1973, reported her birthday accurately, but had her ten years too old. This small sample of dates of birth on post-1969 death certificates casts serious doubt on the reliability of the new system, and on my family's basic numeracy.

Extra details required from the informant of a post-1969 death are the deceased's maiden surname (if a married woman), his/her usual address (in addition to place of death) and place of birth - always treat this item with caution.

OBTAINING CERTIFICATES

1) Register Offices

If you have a good idea of the city, town or village where the birth, marriage or

---

OF MARRIAGE   Given at the GENERAL REGISTER OFFICE, LONDON

Application Number......48.15.G...............

ation District____Manchester____

at The Coll & Parish Church

nchester   in the   County of Lancaster

	Age	Condition	Rank or profession	Residence at the time of marriage	Father's name and surname	Rank or profession of father
	3	4	5	6	7	8
enby	of full age	Bachelor	Spinner	7 Catharine Street London Road	John Gatenby	Carder
rrows	of full age	Spinster	—	54 Jenkinson Street Chorlton upon Medlock	John Barrows	Labourer

according to the rites and Ceremonies of the Established Church after banns by me

Gatenby   in the   ⌈ Mark x of John Barrows   Henry Fielding MA. ⌉
Ann Barrows presence ⌊ Mark x of Henry Barrows   Chaplain ⌋
             of us,

the certified copy of a Register of Marriages in the District above mentioned.

LONDON, under the Seal of the said Office, the   4th   day of   April   19 78

in pursuance of section 65 of the Marriage Act 1949. Sub-section (3) of that section provides that any certified copy of an entry purporting to eal of the General Register Office shall be received as evidence of the marriage to which it relates without any further or other proof of the entry, to have been given in the said Office shall be of any force or effect unless it is sealed or stamped as aforesaid.

) falsifies any of the particulars on this certificate, or (2) uses a falsified certificate as true knowing it to be false, is liable to prosecution.

27: *Marriage certificate - handwritten copy made in 1978.*

ıjor discrepancies between this and the entry in the church register

65

death occurred, you can send £5.50 to that district's Superintendent Registrar, together with brief details of what you want. A personal visit may elicit even more help and advice, but avoid Saturdays (weddings) and Mondays, when the weekend's births and deaths are being registered.

There are 421 registration districts in England and Wales, covering exactly the same areas as one or more borough/district local authorities. You can find the addresses of their Superintendent Registrars in the telephone directory under the heading *Registration of Births, Deaths and Marriages*. The Superintendent Registrars will be listed under *Marriages*: these are the offices where non-current registers are kept. (The *Births and Deaths* offices are only for the purpose of present day registering.)

Alternatively, you can ask for the *Municipal Handbook* (in most libraries) which carries the address of every Superintendent Registrar in the section *District Councils of England and Wales*. The office will do you a five year search in their local indexes. If they can't find the specified entry, they will return your money.

2) The Church

Most 19th Century couples married in the Church of England. If you have an idea of the one at which one your ancestors married, it is usually possible to see the original church register. Figure 28 shows how a marriage register from any Anglican church often becomes freely accessible to the public. Since 1898, the same system has operated in those nonconformist chapels which have opted for *authorised person* status. Roman Catholic churches do not opt for this status, but do normally keep a register of their own.

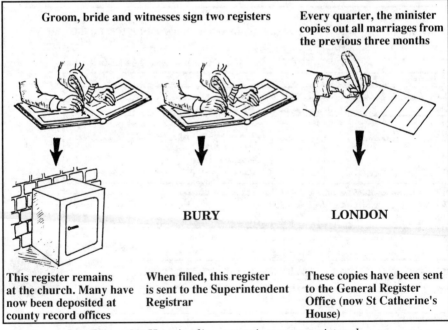

Groom, bride and witnesses sign two registers

Every quarter, the minister copies out all marriages from the previous three months

BURY

LONDON

This register remains at the church. Many have now been deposited at county record offices

When filled, this register is sent to the Superintendent Registrar

These copies have been sent to the General Register Office (now St Catherine's House)

Figure 28: How Anglican marriages are registered

You can almost invariably consult the church register in the county record office, at no charge, and copy out all the details. There may be discrepancies between this and the certificate you get from the GRO. In the example shown on pages 64-5, the original church register gives the bride's name as BORROWS, not BARROWS, and the second witness as Nancy, not Henry. The mother's name of one of my illegitimate ancestors appears under 'father's name' in the church register - the GRO certificate has a blank.

3) St Catherine's House

Most family history researchers must have some dealings with the General Register Office, St Catherine's House (*). Certificates of all birth, marriage and death entries since 1 July 1837 should be available. There are four ways of obtaining such certificates there:

a) Go personally, search the national indexes and order your certificates at £5.50 each - available within four days, though you can pay for a 24 hour service.

b) Write to the GRO Postal Applications Section (*) - £15 per certificate (including a five year search), or £12 if you can supply the index reference.

c) Get somebody living near London to search for and order the certificate you want. (You can contact such people through family history society magazine advertisements. They know the system, and charge only a few pounds for the search.)

d) Use a Mormon Family History Centre to search the national indexes on microfilm (see p77). This method saves valuable time in London, but you still need to use methods **a**, **b** or **c** to obtain the certificate(s). Microfilmed/microfiched copies of the GRO indexes are becoming widely available.

THE NATIONAL INDEXES TO BIRTHS, MARRIAGES AND DEATHS

Any description of the arrangements at the GRO will probably soon be out of date, as plans have been mooted to make microfilmed or microfiched copies of its register entries available for public research. Whatever happens, however, the index system will remain indispensable.

National indexes were compiled in London to the local register entries sent in each quarter by the registrars. They are in large volumes, and are arranged by the quarters - March (covering January-March), June, September and December. Births, marriages and deaths are indexed in separate volumes (red, green and black respectively) in separate parts of the ground floor at St Catherine's House. Blue index volumes refer to overseas registrations.

The index to **births** for the September quarter of 1837 begins like this:

AARON	Mary Ann	Dewsbury	Vol 22	P 37
	Michael	St Geo Southwark	4	78
	Sarah	Dewsbury	22	37
	Sarah	Leicester	15	69
AARONS	Rachel	Whitechapel	2	252
ABBERLEY	Joseph	Stafford	17	89

The Dewsbury entries probably refer to twins.

Starting with the September quarter of 1911, the birth indexes provide the mother's maiden name. My brother's birth is indexed in the December quarter of 1946:

Name	Mother's Maiden Name	Superintendent Registrar's District	Volume	Page
TODD Ian C	GRIFFITHS	Manchester	10e	201

So, if you have a year of birth, you need search four quarters for the entry. Remember that only the name of the registration district is shown in the indexes, and these covered large areas (maybe scores of parishes) - there were over 600 of them in England and Wales in the 19th Century. They were usually named after the largest town or city within them, so you should be able to spot if an entry is right for the area you want. The volume number is a regional code which you can easily follow up on explanatory material at St Catherine's.

Having obtained an entry in the indexes which appears to relate to the birth entry you require, you then complete an application form and submit this at the cash desk together with your fee. The drawback to the current St Catherine's House system is that it is a further four days before the certificate is available for collection; but on the next working day if you pay an extra £14.50 (£20.00 in all).

It is highly likely that you will find more than one John SMITH birth registered in any quarter. If you are after such a birth certificate, you will have to use the 'checking procedure' at St Catherine's House: fill in a 'checking form', writing out all the possible entries you think could be the one you want. Work out which is the most likely, the next most likely and so on, and write them out in that order. (You have to pay a checking fee for personal applications, if more than one has to be checked.) In these circumstances you must have John's father's name so that the GRO staff can identify the correct birth in their registers. If you don't have this, then your first sally into the system must be to obtain John's marriage certificate.

Marriages were indexed under both surnames, so if you are looking for the wedding of Edward GATENBY to Sarah Ann BARROWS, you would never need to use the checking procedure. Once you find an Edward GATENBY entry in a particular quarter, you must find an identical entry under Sarah Ann BARROWS. Otherwise, you can't have the right entry.

Identical entries appear in the December 1837 quarter under their two surnames:

Name	Superintendent Registrar's District	Volume	Page
BARROWS, Sarah Ann	Manchester	XX	338
GATENBY, Edward	Manchester	XX	338

So a marriage certificate, providing ages of the parties and their fathers, leads you to their birth certificates. These, in turn, provide parents' names - and lead you to the next marriage certificate ... and so on, back to 1837, with luck. When searching for the marriage of parents, remember that 25% or more brides were pregnant in the 19th Century, and that children could be born to a couple perhaps 25 years after their wedding.

From the March quarter of 1912, the marriage indexes provide the surname of spouses. June quarter 1941:

| TODD, George (Griffiths) | Manchester | 8d | 133 |
| GRIFFITHS, Annie (Todd) | Manchester | 8d | 133 |

The indexes to **deaths** are the least used volumes in St Catherine's House because of the limited information carried by death certificates. Yet they do have some value :

a) the address could aid a census search.

b) the name of the informant might clinch a relationship.

c) a hereditary disease as cause of death could be a fruitful if worrying piece of evidence.

Applications for death certificates are made in exactly the same way as for birth and marriage certificates. Prior to 1866, the indexes provide only the person's name and the registration district in which death occurred - so John SMITH could have been a few hours old, or a nonagenarian. In such cases, use the checking procedure.

The deaths indexes, however, offer one major piece of information gratis. From the March 1866 quarter onwards they provide ages at death. So where you have an ancestor's year of death, you can ascertain his approximate year of birth without having to buy a death certificate. Search a year or two either way for the birth, since ages at death are very often wrong. From June 1969 the reported date of birth replaces age in the deaths indexes, but the cases of my two grandmothers (see p65) indicate how misleading that can be!

If you are interested in a fairly uncommon surname, the national indexes are sufficiently detailed to provide a lot of information on its bearers without expense. In conjunction with the national index to probate grants (see Chapter 10) some comprehensive pedigrees can be constructed with this data.

PROBLEMS IN OBTAINING CERTIFICATES

Here are the main reasons why you may have trouble obtaining your certificate:

1) Surname variation - although the pronunciation of British surnames had stabilised by the 19th Century, the spelling hadn't. One of the problems that bedevils family historians is that record creation in a pre-literate society relied upon officials writing down what they believed they'd heard. If you were a registrar, how might you have spelt the name AUGHTON, given to you by an agitated, illiterate father, reporting the birth of his thirteenth child, and anxious to get back to work before his pay was docked?

Where the variation from what you expect comes towards the end of the name (NEWBURY instead of NEWBERY, for instance) the entries will be fairly close together in any index, and you should therefore not miss alternative versions. The closer the variation is to the start of the word, the more serious becomes the problem. Such variations may also be less recognisable - whilst searching for NOTLEY, I once passed over several KNOTTLEYs in a parish register before realising that, phonetically, it was the same name. Spelling variations in surnames are like road accidents - they happen to someone else.

Remedy - keep a very open mind, and make a note of the variations for which you have searched. Certain letters - B and P, V and F, D and T - can be the victims of phonetic misrepresentation. One trick is to hold your nose, and repeat the surname - a great eye opener to possible variations.

If you know that a SMITH and JONES each married a ROZHESTVENSKY after 1912, look the marriages up in the indexes under the simpler name. The spouse's surname appears in brackets, so you will be alerted to possible alternative versions which may help in earlier searches. Michael GANDY found his name rendered SANDY when using this technique.

2) **Under registration**- nobody knows how many people were not registered. It was not until 1875 that registration of births and deaths became compulsory - the registration of marriages was in the hands of the officiating clergy or registrar and therefore, as far as the bride and groom were concerned, automatic. Prior to 1875, however, it was not an offence to fail to register a birth or death, unless a registrar had requested you to do so - but since registrars received a fee for registering, they seem to have kept their eyes open. One modern registrar, Chris Ralph, estimates that around 5% slipped through the net (Journal of the Bristol and Avon Family History Society, Winter 1983).

983 deaths of people aged 100+ were registered in 1979. The births of 850 could be traced - another 50 had been born abroad. That left 83 unaccounted for. (A R Thatcher, *Population Trends 25*, Autumn 1981, Office of Population Censuses and Surveys, HMSO.) This suggests a figure closer to 10%.

Remedy - look for births of other children in the family, if your prime concern is the maiden name of the mother; or try to find the parish registers of the church that the family attended. A baptismal entry is proof of parentage.

3) **Flaws in the system** - of the 250,000,000 entries sent in by local registrars since 1837, many thousands must have been lost on route; the compilation of national indexes relied upon copying - cursive Fs and Ts, Ss and Hs could be confused; the staff at St Catherine's are not over particular in dealing with surname variations in their indexes - one gentleman I know was looking for a HATCHETT, found it indexed as HATCHER, filled in the application form accordingly, but had his application returned because (he later established) the name in the register was HATCHETT.

Remedy - try the local register office. They are usually more accommodating.

4) **Wrong name** - people go through life using a second christian name, assiduously concealing the less fashionable first name under which they will appear in the indexes. Some pet names can derive from two or more christian names - Bert from Albert, Bertram or Herbert. One man was universally known as Eddie - his daughter forgot that this was short for Edgar, and so her marriage certificate has him as Edward. (Edmund and Edward seem to suffer similar

interchangeability.) Nicknames cause even greater confusion - my mother-in-law, 'Connie', is really Elizabeth.

This entry, in Harpurhey's burial register, reminds us that it has never been illegal to use an alias:

Army name - Edward WILKINSON Crumpsall 31 July 1876 46yrs

Name - Nebuchadnezzar WORTHINGTON

Remedy - establish the true name, if anybody knows it.

5) **Wrong country** - Scotland, Ireland, the Channel Islands and the Isle of Man have separate systems of civil registration. Indexes are not at St Catherine's House (see pp74-6).

6) **Adoption** - before 1927, there was no legal system of adoption. 'Arrangements were commonly made within the extended family. If you apply for the birth certificate of somebody who was legally adopted after 1 January 1927, it will give you the names of the adopting parents, not the natural parents. The true birth certificate, giving the names of the natural parents, is available only to the adoptee, and only after their 18th birthday. Applicants must attend a counselling session to apprise them of the implications of discovering the true identity of their parents. This system began in 1976. In the ensuing ten years, of the 12,000 who had applied and been counselled, one eighth decided not to proceed; one half pressed on, having obtained their true birth certificate, to try to locate their natural parents.

Since the counselling must take place at St Catherine's House, or in the Social Services Department of the local authority under which the adoptee lives, or where the original adoption order was made, application entails a visit to Britain.

A leaflet, *Tracing the Natural Parents of Adopted Persons*, prepared by Colin Rogers, is available from the Federation of Family History Societies (*) in return for a second class stamp and a stamped addressed envelope.

7) **Problems at the local Register Office** - local applications are often unsuccessful, even though it later transpires that the register office does have a record of the event.

District register offices do not have copies of the national indexes, for these have no relevance to their locally held registers. Registrars index these registers as each one is filled or, in the case of church marriage registers, when they are filled and handed over by the minister.

You can search these local indexes yourself at £15 for six hours, with eight verifications (ie checks in the origin al registers). Sympathetic staff may show you the entry so that you are satisfied that you want a certificate.

Whether you or the staff are searching in the local indexes, the problems can be summarised as follows:

a) The indexes carry less detail than the national one and may even be in calendar form - so if an Isabella ROBSON's birth was registered, an entry, *ROBSON Isabella*, would simply be written on the *R* page of the index. Thus *R* entries are recorded chronologically, not alphabetically, increasing the difficulty of a search.

b) Each sub-district had its own birth and death registers, separately indexed. If you know, from the national indexes, that an ancestor was born in Bury (ie Bury registration district) his birth entry could be in any one of ten separately indexed registers - see the Bury sub-districts on page 42.

c) Modern registration districts usually cover the same areas as one, or two, district council local authorities, and have been in existence only since 1974. These cover areas very different from the old 19th Century registration districts. Old registers have been moved so that each modern registrar has custody of the records of all births, marriages and deaths which have occurred within his present boundary since 1837.

Thus, births, marriages or deaths which are in the national indexes under Bury may have occurred in sub-districts whose registers now belong to another register office.

d) Each church's marriages would also be separately indexed. So, if you know from the St Catherine's House indexes that a marriage took place in Bolton in the first quarter of 1870, it could be necessary to search the local indexes to the dozens of churches in the registration district. The search could be even longer if you know only that the marriage occurred 'somewhere around Bolton in the 1870s'.

e) Some churches have never deposited registers with a Superintendent Registrar. Look back to the figure 28 (p66). The Superintendent Registrar only gets his copy of a church's marriage register when all 500 blanks are filled. This can take years. Some small rural churches are still on the register they started in 1837.

f) Marriage registers, too, have had to be moved, especially since 1974, to accommodate boundary changes - but the surgery has not always been so clinically easy.

Take Oswaldtwistle in Lancashire, once in Blackburn but now in the registration district of Hyndburn and Rossendale. Formerly, Oswaldtwistle people who married at the register office did so at Blackburn. Their entries are in the register of Blackburn register office marriages which has of course remained at Blackburn despite the boundary changes.

This also applies to weddings in non-Anglican Oswaldtwistle churches - before 1898, registrars had to be present to register such nonconformist (including Roman Catholic) marriages. These too are in the Blackburn office register. Figure 29 indicates that many townships in the Blackburn area alone have been similarly affected by boundary changes.

Remedy - use the GRO, or try adjacent registration district offices.

The *Ordnance Survey Administrative Area Diagrams* (scale 1:100,000) show modern local authority boundaries (on which registration districts are based) and are in central libraries.

8) **Incorrect certificates** - since 1986, fraudulent use of certificates has been countered by the introduction of fluorescent banding. False statements to registrars were once punishable by transportation. Unfortunately, the moral (if not legal) equivalent of such fraud has gone on for years in the shape of the issue of incorrectly copied certificates. Dangers arise at local register offices, which do not have the technology to photocopy original register entries onto certificates. But the GRO also relies on some hand copying, and its standard of accuracy is low.

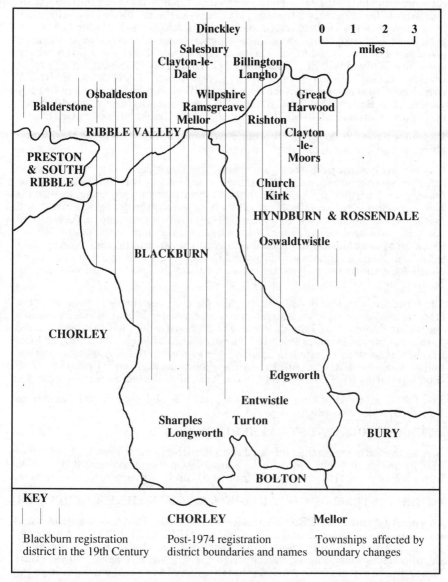

Figure 29: Blackburn registration district's boundary changes

Dinckley

Salesbury
Clayton-le-
Dale

Billington
Langho

0   1   2   3

miles

Osbaldeston

Wilpshire
Ramsgreave
Mellor

Great
Harwood

Balderstone

Rishton

RIBBLE VALLEY

Clayton
-le-
Moors

PRESTON
& SOUTH
RIBBLE

Church
Kirk

HYNDBURN & ROSSENDALE

Oswaldtwistle

BLACKBURN

CHORLEY

Edgworth

Entwistle

Sharples   Turton
Longworth

BURY

BOLTON

KEY

CHORLEY   Mellor

Blackburn registration   Post-1974 registration   Townships affected by
district in the 19th Century district boundaries and names boundary changes

Many of the errors are innocuous - like the Manchester 'Lurryman' of 1875 who
had become a 'Quarryman' (in a city centre!) by 1878. However, this is nothing
to the experience of a researcher who found on one certificate a tanner of Upper
Moon with the christian name Polwasab. Checking the parish register baptism,
she found him to be a farmer of Upper Moor, named Edward! (Kent FHS Journal,
vol IV, no 12.) My recent experiences (I have had to return a marriage certificate

twice to get it to tally with what I know to be in the parish register entry) have convinced me that in the case of hand written certificates issued by the GRO, their declaration 'Certified to be a true copy of an entry in the certified copy of a Register of Marriages in the District above mentioned' is worthless. I wonder how many thousands of family historians have sought wrong addresses in the census (Wesham Square, Sunderland, instead of Nesham Square) or even wrong ancestors (William Will ROBSON instead of William Lill ROBSON) on account of careless copying? Most serious of all - wrong surnames - BARTON for BARLOW (which held up a cousin of mine for years); or the Yorkshire researcher who happily pursued the Bolton Abbey family of GILL on the strength of a hand written certificate, until a relative told him that the name should have been GAIL!

Remedy - if ever in doubt about a hand written certificate, write to the issuing office, or GRO, or both, to query the accuracy.

9) **Absolutely stumped** - then go overseas. Foreign systems of civil registration are often more comprehensive than our own, and may provide information about an ancestor's brother or cousin which can help with earlier generations. I have a New York State death certificate of 1907 which records the deceased's father and mother (with maiden name) so leading back easily to a marriage in Yorkshire in 1823. Victoria death certificates include this *and* the names and ages of all the deceased's issue. Mass emigration from Britain began around 1840, and by 1914 some 19 million had gone overseas beyond Europe, the favourite destination being North America (three million went there during the peak period of 1845-55). So everybody in Britain has foreign relatives.

10) **London** is uniquely difficult terrain for civil registration research - the crowd of people, together with an intermixture of nationalities and accents, makes the national indexes so difficult to use. Parish registration, which has continued parallel to the civil system since 1837, is an essential lifeline. Webb (**27, 28** - use in conjunction with **15**, cited on page 51) shows boundaries of Anglican parishes and registration districts. (All three are available, at £2.40 each (incl p&p) from the West Surrey FHS, 17 Lane End Drive, Knaphill, Woking, Surrey GU21 2QQ.)

The fullest analysis of civil registration problems and possible solutions is in Rogers (**5**) (full reference on page 23).

OTHER RECORDS AT ST CATHERINE'S HOUSE

Also at the GRO are births and deaths, on British registered craft, at sea (since 1837) or in the air (since 1949); births, marriages and deaths amongst the armed forces (some from 1761, but mainly from 1881) and of British subjects overseas.

OTHER SYSTEMS OF CIVIL REGISTRATION IN THE BRITISH ISLES

Channel Islands - GUERNSEY (including Alderney, Herm, Jethou and Sark) civil registration of births and deaths began in 1840, and for Sark and Alderney in 1925; Anglican marriages were centrally registered only after 1919. Certificates can be obtained by post from the Registrar General, Royal Court House (*) at a cost of £5.00. Apply to churches (list of addresses available from the Registrar General) for earlier marriages.

JERSEY - the system began in 1842. Certificates cost £5.00. The postal handling charge for applications from the UK is 50p; £5.00 is charged for a five year search for a birth or death and £10.00 for a five year marriage search. There are no facilities for personal research. Write to the Superintendent Registrar at Royal Square (*).

Ireland - full civil registration in Ireland began on 1 January 1864, although registration of marriages other than those celebrated by a Catholic priest had begun on 1 April 1845. (This, of course, excluded the vast majority, but included all Protestant denominations.) Much Irish civil registration research can now be done at Mormon Family History Centres (see p77). Most researchers wanting actual certificates will need to make postal applications to the following addresses:

1) The General Register Office, Joyce House, 8-11, Lombard St East, Dublin 2 (tel: 0001 (from UK) 671 1000)

2) The General Register Office, Oxford House, 49-55, Chichester St, Belfast BT1 4HL (tel: 0232 526942). **Address to change mid-1994.**

The following table uses these numbers as a location code for where to apply:

	Eire (Southern Ireland - the '26 counties')	Ulster (Northern Ireland - the '6 counties'*)	
	1 Jan 1864 - present	1 Jan 1864 - 31 Dec 1921	1 Jan 1922 - present
Births & Deaths	1	1 & 2	2
Marriages	1 (Non- RC commence 1 April 1846)	1**	2

*   Antrim, Armagh, Down, Fermanagh, Londonderry and Tyrone.
** District Registration Offices, covering areas co-terminous with the 26 borough/ district local authorities, also hold these registers. Write to (2) for a list of their addresses.

Irish registration before 1874 was even more erratic than that in England and Wales, especially of births and deaths. Some Catholic priests were not conscientious in sending their marriage registers to Dublin. Joyce House, Dublin will undertake a five year search for a birth, marriage or death and issue a certificate for IR£5.50, but specify that you need only a photocopy and the charge is just IR£3.00. The information recorded is the same as that on English and Welsh certificates. Various other registers are held at Joyce House - for example births and deaths at sea, abroad, and adoptions from 10 July 1953 - the start of legalised adoption in Eire.

Oxford House, Belfast, operates the same system as obtains in England - they will only provide information in the format of certificates which cost (1 July 1992) £5.50, other than a free 'search only' service to confirm a date of birth. Adoption records for Northern Ireland are also at Oxford House - the system began in 1931.

Indexes to Irish registration are **not** at St Catherine's House. Both general register offices in Ireland will send you a leaflet giving details of their holdings, charges, and other avenues of Irish research.

Isle of Man - the system has operated since 1878 (marriages from 1884). No entries will be found in the St Catherine's House indexes. Write to the General Registry, Douglas (*). Certificates cost £5.50 and a search fee of £2.00 per year is charged. The Adoption Register dates from 1928. A list of local professional researchers is available from the General Registry.

Scotland - civil registration began on 1 January 1855. The easiest way to obtain a certificate is by writing to the General Register Office for Scotland (*). The charge is now £12.00, and this includes a five year search (ie two years before and after the year specified). Note, however, how the Mormons can help (see p77).

Scottish certificates are very detailed. Apart from the years 1856-60 inclusive, they carry additionally to the information on English and Welsh certificates:

Birth certificate - date and place of parents' marriage.

Marriage certificate - names and maiden names of the groom's and bride's mothers.

Death certificate - marital condition, parents' names and occupation of father.

The initial enthusiasm of the authorities meant that during the first year of registration (1855) registrars had to collect a wealth of information - for example. birth registers carry the birthplaces of both parents, and details of any other children that the father had sired. The death registers give place of burial. Regrettably it proved impossible to sustain so exhaustive a system of registration.

It is worth visiting New Register House for at least two reasons:

1) For payment of a fee (currently £16.00 per day) it is possible to consult the Scottish civil registration indexes on computer and then look at self-access microfiche copies of the registers. You can copy down the entries for nothing.

2) Scottish census returns and Old Parish Registers (ie pre-1855) are available in the same building. A day's search in all three types of record costs the £16.00 mentioned above; a week's search is £60.00. The Register of Neglected Entries (1801-54) comprises births, marriages and deaths proved, after 1855, to have occurred in Scotland but not entered in the Old Parish Registers.

The indexes to Scottish civil registration are held on microfilm at various locations in England and Wales - the Society of Genealogists (*) (write for details of access to their massive holdings) and at many Mormon Family History Centres (see p77). Scottish indexes are **not** held at St Catherine's House. In both marriage and death indexes, women are double indexed under maiden and married name. Scottish adoption records, also at New Register House, date from 1930.

Searches can also be made in the registers at local register offices, but the two-hourly charge of £10.00 now makes this facility expensive.

New Register House will send you useful leaflets giving details of opening times, charges, other record holdings, and addresses at which to contact professional researchers.

For **European** ancestry, see Law (**26**).

DIVORCE

There were just 24 in 1858, the first year that divorce was possible other than by private Act of Parliament, but 151,000 in 1989. Divorce has become a practical option for ordinary people only in the 20th Century. The decree absolute gives the date and place of the marriage being dissolved. The Record Keeper of the Divorce Registry (*) will search the national index (£5.00 for up to 10 years) and provide a copy of the decree. Personal applications will only trigger a three year while-you-wait search, so it is better to apply postally. If you have the case number, apply direct to the relevant court (fee £1.00). There is no public access to the indexes.

For records of Manx divorces, contact the General Registry (*).

Records of Ulster divorces are at the Royal Courts of Justice, Belfast BT1 3JF.

The Irish Republic does not permit divorce.

Records of Scottish divorces (from May 1984) are at the General Register Office for Scotland (*). For earlier cases, apply to the Court of Session (*).

THE MORMON CHURCH

The Mormons take great interest in family history for doctrinal reasons. They have many branch libraries (called Family History Centres) in the UK, attached to their churches - addresses in telephone directories under *Church of Jesus Christ of Latter Day Saints*. Non-Mormons are welcome to use these library facilities. No attempt will be made to convert you, but do not offend their religious views by taking in tobacco, flasks of tea, coffee or alcohol!

Many of these branch libraries will have:

a) a portion of the national indexes of English and Welsh civil registration (1837-1980) on numerous microfilms (and increasingly on fiche) available otherwise only at St Catherine's House and some libraries and record offices.

b) the national indexes of Scottish civil registration (1855-1955) and the actual registers for 1855-75, 1881 and 1891 - all on microfilm.

c) **the indexes of Irish** civil registration (up to 1958/9); and the registers up to 1870 (marriages and deaths), and for births 1864-81 and 1900-13, with some post 1922 coverage - again, all on microfilm.

d) the International Genealogical Index - all branches will have this. It is a county by county index of parish registers, expanded every few years. It is on microfiche. Although primarily a tool for the pre-1837 period, baptisms and marriages up to the 1880s also figure in it. It is an index and the original source must be consulted - a church baptismal or marriage register. This will be usually at the relevant county record office but some are still with the church incumbent. His address can be obtained from Crockford's *Clerical Directory*, available in most libraries. A more detailed description of the IGI will figure in a future book in this series.

FURTHER READING

25 *Index to Registration Districts* (General Register Office for Scotland). Lists all Scottish registration districts, with changes (£2 +p&p from the GRO for S (*))

26 Hugh T Law, *How to trace your Ancestors in Europe* (Cottonwood Books). $16.00 from 1216 Lillie Circle, Salt Lake City, Utah 84121, USA

27 Cliff Webb, *Genealogical Research in Victorian London* (West Surrey FHS, 1993)

28 Cliff Webb, *Genealogical Research in Late Victorian and Edwardian London* (West Surrey FHS, 1994). Indicates the new parishes created after c1870

10 WILLS: 1858 TO THE PRESENT

NOT IN MY FAMILY!

A person's last will and testament is an especially personal document. Yet within months of his or her death its contents are readily available for scrutiny by any member of the public, related or not. Once accepted as authentic by the State, a will becomes an important legal document, able to influence human activity decades and even centuries after the death of its author. Therefore, the State (and before 1858 the Church) has taken elaborate steps to secure the survival of every will that has ever been authenticated.

Many people starting their family history refuse to believe that their ancestors could ever have left wills, and therefore that this class of record could ever be relevant to their research. They are always wrong:

1) Up to 10% of the population left wills prior to this century. This figure is now about 35%.

2) Uncles, aunts, great uncles, great aunts and cousins may have left wills which name your ancestors and specify relationships.

3) Most wills name around ten people, usually relatives, and often spanning three generations. I have encountered an 1840 example in which 40 of the testator's relatives were named.

4) The economic changes of the last two centuries have produced much upward social mobility - so even very humble stock may have wealthy, will-making relatives. There has also been much downward social mobility - labouring families in industrial towns may descend from solid landowning yeoman stock or craftsmen who had sufficient possessions to consider will-making vital.

THE VALUE OF WILLS

1) The genealogical information contained in wills is of obvious value. Those who make them (testators and testatrixes) usually name many members of the family who are to benefit from their decease, and may also specify those who are not to. Anticipation of death, however, can calm even the most vindictive spirit and amends may be made - family black sheep and skeletons such as errant brothers, illegitimate children and grandchildren, and other unspeakables may at last be acknowledged.

2) Wills provide the most cast-iron evidence available to family historians for ascertaining precise relationships within family groups. We've already seen that major sources like census returns can mislead in this respect. Phrases like 'to my children Daniel, John and Mary that I had by my first wife Sarah' cannot be much clearer.

3) Wills, like families, know no geographical bounds. They may name relatives in different (and possibly ancestral) parts of the country or world.

4) They may name children, nephews or nieces whose existence you had never suspected. This may alert you to collateral lines of descent (ie descendants from ancestors other than your own direct line). These can often be traced forwards through trades directories, electoral registers and then modern telephone directories. Living representatives of these collateral lines may have important genealogical information or documents (especially family bibles).

5) Bachelor and spinster members of the family are often more likely to make wills because there is no obvious heir to their property. Such wills are likely to name brothers, sisters, nephews, nieces and cousins. One 1865 unmarried testator that I unearthed named 13 cousins. Such a clue can lace together otherwise isolated entries in census returns and parish registers to reconstitute a man's full family tree.

6) Wills give very personal insight into wealth and status - in the shape of legacies like 'my watch', or 'my shares in the Manchester Ship Canal Company', a reference which could be followed up in the company share register. Legatees might include 'my servant' or 'my housekeeper'.

7) Prior to the 1882 Married Women's Property Act, a wife's property became vested in her husband at marriage. So, before 1882, only spinsters, widows, and married women who had their husbands' consent left wills. To retain some independence for their daughter's property, a bride's parents often concluded a marriage agreement or settlement with the groom. Although these were private agreements, and not therefore registered anywhere, they are often referred to in women's (and men's) wills. They were often signed immediately before a wedding day, and so their dates, when mentioned, can be a valuable pointer.

8) Precise references to real estate (buildings and land) can lead to other sources. A family shop, business or farm could be traced in trade directories, rate books or Land Tax assessments. The latter are held at county record offices, and usually run from 1780 to 1832. Earlier holders of the property could be ancestral. HM Land Registry (*) will identify the current owners for you, and they *might* co-operate in giving you access to the property deeds.

References to 'all my copyhold land which I hold from the manor of Tottington' naturally lead to manorial court records. Many manorial courts continued to sit twice yearly up to 1925, acting as modern land registries in that they recorded inheritance, sale or mortgage of property. This is a specialised topic, unsuitable for the beginner in family history, but it is possible to locate the whereabouts of such records. This could be a county record office or the solicitor who still acts as steward to the manor to protect surviving mineral rights. Family ownership of a property may have spanned centuries, and could be recorded as surrenders and admittances in the court books or court rolls.

To summarise, wills can unblock many genealogical dead ends - witness the numerous articles written in family history society magazines under the cruelly flogged title 'Where there's a will there's a way'.

A SHORT CUT TO FINDING A WILL

If you have post-1858 dates of death for any ancestors, your easiest starting point is to write for a few RK1 forms from The Probate Sub-Registry, York (*). You need one per person to make a request to ascertain whether a grant of probate was ever made for his/her estate. Include the full name, the date of death and address (as fully as possible). A three year search from the date of death you provide will be made, for a charge of £2.00 per will or admon. If this is successful, you will be sent a photocopy. Stress that you want all the probate documents relating to the grant.

Unfortunately, the service is slow - the Sub-Registry currently advises that a search is subject to n weeks delay!

THE LIFE STORY OF A POST-1858 WILL

Stages

1) The testator (female - testatrix) wrote it out (a holographic will) or, more likely, had it drawn up by a solicitor.

Important Genealogical Considerations

A will always reflects the situation at the time of writing, and could have been drawn up years before the testator's death. During this time legatees could have died, but this rarely warranted the drawing up of any amendment (called a codicil).

This is the last Will and Testament of me George Smethurst of Broad Street, Pendleton near Manchester Tripe Dresser

2) The testator included in the will the name(s) of its executor(s) who were to carry out the instructions contained within it.

Executor(s) were normally close relatives, often the principal beneficiaries; solicitors increasingly performed this function on behalf of the executors.

And I appoint my friend Edward Kelly of Medlock Street Hulme and my nephew Joseph Smethurst of Pendleton Executors and Trustees

3) The testator signed the will in the presence of two witnesses, or made his mark.

Witnesses to the signature were likely to be close neighbours, or a solicitor and his clerk, since beneficiaries of the will were debarred.

his
George X Smethurst
mark

4) After the testator's death, an executor took the will to the Principal Probate Registry (Somerset House) or to a District Probate Registry.

District probate registries were set up in important centres with jurisdiction over specified areas, usually one or more counties. Populous counties (eg Lancashire and Yorkshire) were sub-divided and therefore had more than one registry. In 1926, such jurisdictions were removed, and executors could use any probate registry.

Stages	Important Genealogical Considerations
5) Having satisfied itself that the will was genuine, the registry issued a grant of probate. This was written at the foot of the will, or on its back, together with the testator's date of death. It retained the original will, made a registered copy (up to 1940) in a volume for its own use and forwarded another copy to the Principal Probate Registry (Somerset House).	It follows that there are at least two copies of every will proved at any District Probate Registry - one there, and one at Somerset House. In the case of London and the nearby counties, all wills were proved at the Principal Probate Registry, so that Somerset House holds all copies. The Principal Probate Registry moved to Llandudno in World War II.

Proved at Manchester the 20 day of November 1890 by the oaths of Edwin Kelly (in the Will written Edward Kelly) and Joseph Smethurst the Nephew the Executors to whom Administration was granted

The Testator George Smethurst was late of N° 231 Broad Street Pendleton near Manchester in the County of Lancaster Super.

6) The executor(s) used a further copy of the will to execute its terms.	The executors' copy occasionally survives amongst a family's papers. If a family solicitor acted as executor, his archives may contain other useful family documents. It is possible to locate the practice or its successor through a telephone directory or through the Law Society.

LETTERS OF ADMINISTRATION

Until 1939, a person could will personal property to anybody he/she wished, and had equal freedom with real estate, with the exception of land held by certain types of tenure.

Where a person left no will (ie died intestate), the law has always laid down very precisely who should gain the estate. Most people, however, have had experience of the smooth partitioning of a dead relative's property without recourse to law. The surviving partner takes over the deceased's property without dispute. Where there is no partner, a division takes place amongst the children without any need to obtain probate, though usually with sufficient acrimony to spark or fuel a family feud.

Legal authority to administer an intestate's estate has been necessary where sizeable amounts of property are involved, or where ownership of bank accounts, shares and the like must be transferred. A close relative, usually the surviving partner, or a son or daughter, or their solicitor, would apply to a Probate Registry for Letters of Administration (commonly abbreviated to Admon). These bound the relative (the administrator) to allocate the estate according to a strict formula.

After 1925, a surviving spouse had a first charge of £1,000 on the estate, plus a life interest in half the residue and in all if there were no children. (This *statutory legacy* of £1,000 has been regularly increased, and reached £70,000 in June 1987.) Subsequent rights to the estate are shown, in order of priority, on this diagram:

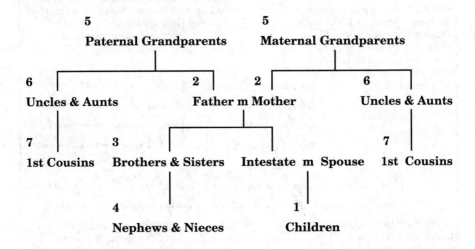

Where no such relative exists, the estate goes to the Crown. Before 1925, the law was slightly different: a distinction was made between real and personal property, widowers had more rights than widows, and remoter relatives could be eligible for the estate.

Clearly, some very careful genealogy had to be researched to wind up some estates. Consequently, very detailed pedigrees, annotated with fractions to indicate due shares, together with accounts of moneys distributed, may survive amongst family papers or with the family solicitor (see p81).

Most researchers, however will find that only a copy of the Letters of Administration survive at the District Probate Registry. A copy was also sent to Somerset House, in exactly the same way as with wills. Admons carry only the barest outline of genealogical information:

1) the full name of the deceased

2) his/her usual address

3) occupation (or marital condition in the case of a woman)

4) the date and place of death

5) the full name, address and occupation of the administrator

6) his/her relationship to the deceased

7) the gross value of the estate and

8) the value of the estate after the payment of death duty.

Although only one 'next of kin' normally applied for letters of administration, his/her accompanying declaration could be of interest. For example:

1) 'the lawful daughter and one of the persons entitled to share in the estate'

2) 'the lawful daughter and only next of kin'

3) 'the lawful cousin german' (ie first cousin) the intestate dying 'without parent brother or sister uncle or aunt nephew or niece'.

Death Duty Registers will identify the unnamed beneficiaries, and indicate their relationships to the intestate, in the case of admons granted before 1894 (see p86).

Often, the name of the solicitors who acted for the applicant will be given on the admon, after the words 'extracted by ...'. It is worth following up this reference (see p81).

Anybody interested in the intricacies of probate law should see Bailey (**29**).

THE NATIONAL INDEX OF WILLS AND ADMONS, 1858 TO PRESENT

This is formally known as the *Calendar of the Grants of Probate and Letters of Administration made in the Probate Registries of the High Court of Justice.* It covers only England and Wales, although the few 'resealings' in England of any Irish, Scottish and colonial wills are also included.

This massive and ever growing animal lives at the Principal Probate Registry (*) Somerset House in London, where it is available for public use at no charge. Each year since 1858, all grants of probate and administration have been indexed alphabetically by surname and within each surname by christian name. A year's grants run into several volumes. Since 1973, the annual index has been produced in microfiche form. Admons were indexed in separate volumes from 1858 to 1870.

Fortunately for provincials, duplicate sets are kept at District Probate Registries. These are working offices, however, and access to the index is not so readily guaranteed as at Somerset House because:

1) The index volumes over 50 years in age have often been deposited at the nearest county record office. For precise details of your local situation see Gibson (**30**), the cheapest and most readily obtainable work on the terminology and location of probate records of the post-1858 and pre-1858 periods.

2) Although there is no charge for searching, the volumes at the district registries are often housed in dingy side rooms. A phone call will ascertain whether they are always available for researchers (see Gibson (**30**) for addresses; telephone directory entries are under *Probate Sub-Registry* or *Probate Registry*).

The national index is a very valuable tool for family historians for four reasons:

1) An RK1 application is unlikely to be successful if you don't have a precise date of death or address.

2) The index is easier to use than the national index to deaths at St Catherine's House, as entries are more detailed and more readily identifiable. There is only one volume to search for each year, not four, so it is also a short cut to tracing a death, if you are fairly certain that a will or admon was involved.

3) Some information - addresses of executors (given before 1892), their occupations (given until 1967) and the value of estate - may not appear in the actual will.

4) The entries are sufficiently detailed to act as family history resource material in their own right:

a) Before 1 January 1892, entries gave relationships of executors to the deceased if they were related:

1891 Will £484 3s 5d	**Gatenby** John late of Leyburn Yorkshire Tinplate Worker died 17th Dec 1890 at Leyburn probate granted at the **Principal Probate Registry** 27th Feb 1891 to Mary Gatenby of the same place widow and relict and John Garth Gatenby of Leyburn General Dealer and son executors.

b) Entries after 1 January 1892 do not give relationships of executors to the testator, or the executor' addresses:

1907 Will	**Gatenby** John Garth late of Leyburn Yorkshire died 21st April 1907 at Leyburn probate granted at the **Principal Probate Registry** to Mary Brown Gatenby widow William Anton Stamp Distributor and Christopher Smithson Photographer. Effects £2,476 17s 8d.*

c) Entries indicating grant of letters of administration are equally detailed:

1865 Administration under £100	**Gatenby** Mary late of Carthorpe Yorkshire widow died 16th March 1865 administration granted at **York** 19th April 1865 to John Gatenby of Leyburn Yorkshire Tinner son one of the next of kin.

*[Note that Mary Brown GATENBY may have been the widow of the testator, but the entry does not specify this.]

Some tips for using the national indexes:

1) The volumes are heavy, but you can abstract all references to one relatively uncommon surname in say one county over a period of half a century in one afternoon.

2) Where you have a few surnames to search, work on them in alphabetical groups so that you are taking down only one volume per year - ARKWRIGHTs and BENTLEYs, for instance, are almost always in the same volume, whatever the year.

This way, you will proceed quickly, spot the same families reappearing, and feel that you are getting somewhere. Blanket searches involving several volumes are a slow grind.

3) Ages at death, not provided in probate records, are freely available from the post-1866 indexes to deaths at St Catherine's House. This extra information will help to tie in testators with your other findings.

The national index to grants of probate is now available on microfilm at some record offices, and at Mormon Family History Centres from 1858-1957, with several years of each letter on one film. This accelerates any search and is a great advance, but by the end of this century I hope the Mormons will have created a consolidated index by merging all entries from 1858 to the present into one alphabetical sequence. That will save researchers millions of hours of lifting and searching.

GAINING ACCESS TO WILLS

Having found entries in the national index, there are three ways of seeing the actual wills and admons:

1) Ordering photocopies from the Probate Sub-Registry, York (see p79).

2) Going to Somerset House (see map, p93) open weekdays 10.00am-4.30pm. You can see each will or admon for a small charge. However, you must carry the relevant index volume to the counter to allow the staff to copy out the index entry onto an application form. 'Last orders' are 4-15pm. You can make an abstract, but cannot trace signatures - so, at 25p per page for personal applications, you may as well order a photocopy, provided within five working days.

3) In the case of wills proved in the last 50 years, copies should be at the District Probate Registry where the original grant was made. You can look at the will or admon at no charge, but it should be remembered that this is something of a cinderella service in government eyes, and in my experience some of the registries are under-staffed. Consequently, a phone call is advisable - wills may only be produced at certain times, and by appointment. District Registries often deposit their probate records over 50 years old in the local county record office. Gibson (**30**) gives county by county details, but the situation could easily change at any particular registry - again, enquire before visiting.

Some district registries have retained their copy wills and admons back to 1858.

The Mormons are currently (1994) microfilming all probate grants from 1858 to 1925, and these should be available through their Family History Centres soon.

WHAT SHOULD I RECORD?

Even if you order a photocopy of a will, you must eventually make an abstract of its contents. Otherwise, its genealogical information remains coded and difficult to retrieve quickly.

Having wrestled with wills from the 16th to the 20th Centuries, I reckon that they have enough common features to be filleted and put onto the standard form which I designed. Despite my vested interest, I believe that these will record sheets are the easiest (and quickest) way of abstracting and storing will-content. See page 12 for how to obtain them.

Ironically, 19th and 20th Century wills are easier to read than their earlier ancestors, but harder to understand. This seems to be a direct result of testators increasingly using lawyers to draw up their wills and testaments:

1) Solicitors were paid by written mileage. Oddly enough, this tended to increase the length of wills!

2) Legal advice led to increased use of trusts. By the late 19th Century, even small tradesmen, once happy to bequeath their stock, tools, household items and cash simply and without fuss, now insisted on appointing trustees to 'sell and convert the same into money either by public auction or private contract at such times and in such manner as they think fit (with power to rescind any contract for sale)'! With such material to work on, it is not surprising that solicitors' clerks could easily-clock three or four pages where formerly one would have done.

DEATH DUTY REGISTERS 1796-1894

Admons give few details about beneficiaries, and some wills may frustratingly refer only to 'my loving wife and all my children'. Fortunately, legacy duty was payable, and details were carefully logged down in large death duty registers (class no IR26), now held at the Public Record Office, Chancery Lane (*). Between 1815 and 1853, it was paid by every beneficiary, except the spouse, on legacies or residues of over £20 if the estates were worth over £100. At other times, different exceptions have applied.

The registers give the names of these beneficiaries and their consanguinity - ie their blood relationship to the deceased, since this determined the rate of duty. A code was used - DBF meant descendant of a brother of a father, GG child - a great grandchild. Details of the code, and much other useful information, are in the PRO leaflet No 34, *The Death Duty Registers*, available free by post from the PRO.

These registers were 'active' for 50 years and notes were made in them of the deaths of, or whereabouts of beneficiaries. They can be most illuminating - 'died upwards of 15 years ago', or 'in America, presumed dead' for example.

Where a date of probate is known, it is worth writing to the PRO to obtain photocopies of the relevant death duty register entries.

Indexes to the registers are on open shelf in the wills room of the PRO at Chancery Lane, under the class no IR27. They are a useful finding aid for wills proved before 1858, when probate was administered through some 300 church courts.

When it is likely that someone did leave a will in the period 1796-1858, these indexes will give the court and date of probate; the will is likely to be at a county record office. About a quarter of probates were liable for duty between 1796 and 1805, about three quarters from 1805 to 1815, and thereafter nearly all.

People unable to visit London can get paid research done by writing to the PRO for a list of searchers. Alternatively, most family history societies can now put you in touch with a London searcher.

PROBATE VALUATIONS

The value of the deceased's estate appears in the national indexes, on all letters of administration and was often written at the foot of a will by the probate registry.

Before 1881, this value will rarely be given as an exact figure, but rather in the form 'under £100' or some similarly rounded sum.

The valuations are gross, and do not take into account the necessary payments of personal debts and funeral expenses.

The value of real estate (buildings and land) did not appear before 1898, unless it was freehold property rented out for a fixed number of years.

OTHER COUNTRIES IN THE BRITISH ISLES

Channel Islands - separate wills had to be made for the bequest of realty (immovable property such as buildings and lands) as opposed to personalty (movable goods, including money and credits).

GUERNSEY (including Alderney, Herm and Sark) - for realty the Greffe, Royal Court House, St Peter Port, Guernsey; for personalty - the Registrar, Ecclesiastical Court, Constables' Office, St Peter Port, Guernsey.

JERSEY - Judicial Greffier, 16 Hill Street, St Helier, Jersey.

Ireland - EIRE - civil probate was introduced in 1858, at the same time as in England and Wales. Grants could be granted at:

1) District registries - a copy was retained there and the original sent to the Principal Registry in Dublin.

2) The Principal Registry, Dublin.

All the pre-1904 original wills in the Principal Registry at Dublin were destroyed in the fire of 1922. A few of the original district registry wills sent to Dublin survived.

The National Archives of Ireland (*) holds all original wills of 1904-73 (ie over 20 years old) together with the district registry copies of most wills proved since 1858. Wills remain with the registry at which they were proved for 20 years. The National Archives similarly holds papers relating to admons for1904-73 if granted at the Principal Registry, and for 1900-73 if granted at a district registry.

Annual, alphabetical calendars of all wills and admons since 1858 are available in the reading room of the National Archives.

Ireland - NORTHERN IRELAND - the Public Record Office of Northern Ireland (*) holds copy wills for the province from 1858.

Isle of Man - post-1910 wills, and deeds to Manx property, are at The Deeds Registry, in the General Registry, Douglas (*). For 1628 to 1910 these records are at The Manx Museum and National Trust, Kingswood Grove, Douglas, Isle of Man.

Scotland - known as testaments, wills have since the 1820s been proved at a sheriff's court - roughly, each one covers a pre-1974 shire. The courts retain their testaments and testaments dative (ie admons) for 20-30 years, before depositing them at the Scottish Record Office (*). Orkney and Shetland retain their records at local archives. A unified index to all Scottish grants of probate, the *Calendar of Confirmations and Inventories*, runs from 1876 to the present, and can be referred to at the Scottish Record Office. From the 1820s to 1875, each court's grants have a separate index at the Scottish Record Office.

Prior to the 1820s, probate was administered by 22 courts, known as commissary courts because they were relics of the pre-Reformation diocesan courts of the Catholic church. Indexes for the years 1800 to the 1820s (when sheriffs courts took over this function) are at the Scottish Record Office. Indexes prior to 1800 (in many cases going back to the 16th Century) were published by the Scottish Record Society around 1900, and are available in libraries, as well as at the SRO.

SRO Leaflet No 19, *Indexes in the Historical Search Room to Deeds, Sasines and Testamentary Records* is available gratis by post.

FURTHER READING

29 SJ Bailey, *The Law of Wills* (Pitman,1973)

30 Jeremy Gibson, *A Simplified Guide to Probate Jurisdiction* (FFHS,1985)

31 Cecil J Sinclair, *Tracing your Scottish Ancestors* (HMSO,1990). A detailed guide to the Scottish Record Office - available from there (*) at £7.74 incl p&p

11 WHERE NEXT?

FAMILY HISTORY SOCIETIES

Virtually every county in Britain has at least one family history society. Common characteristics are:

1) Monthly meetings at one venue or more.

2) A quarterly magazine to which members submit articles on their own research discoveries and difficulties, and appeal for, or offer help with specific surnames.

3) Cheap annual subscriptions - £10.00 or less.

4) Annual conferences, featuring lectures on sources, research and specialised topics relating to family history.

5) Directories of members' research surname interests. Members almost invariably find someone in a society who is chasing the same name as themselves in a particular town or village.

6) Facilities for reciprocal research - you research in London for a Lancashire member and vice versa, to overcome problems of travelling. A sophisticated example of this is the 'Link' service offered by one Yorkshire society whereby a document can be researched almost anywhere in the country by a member volunteer in return for expenses.

7) A range of typed up projects - 1851 census indexes, marriage indexes, transcriptions of graveyard MIs (monumental inscriptions). These will be available for members' use. Some societies have a policy of publishing such material.

Few people live in the county of their ancestors. Exiles will find that a county society's magazine provides local knowledge on sources, record offices and members' research findings. Most societies now acknowledge that many if not most of their members are 'out of county' and therefore try to provide for them some kind of simple query-answering service.

There is a strong case for joining the society which serves the area in which you live, even if you can claim no local ancestors. The monthly meetings allow you to mix with fellow members who will range from the reticent beginner to the communicative and well-informed expert and on to the irrepressible obsessive whose life revolves around a roll of pedigree-embossed wallpaper. George Pelling, an eminent writer and speaker on family history, came to Lancashire from Sussex at the whim of his Inland Revenue employers, joined the old Rossendale Society for Genealogy & Heraldry, and became one of its most active members, despite the fact that none of his ancestors had ever been further north than Petworth in Sussex!

Ironically, family history societies are rarely run by active researchers. As research avenues get blocked or involve more travel, once eager and enthusiastic members lose their hunger for findings and sink into the morass known as 'the committee'. Here they sublimate their original curiosity about their own families into the ceaseless administrative grind of operating a society which helps others do what they no longer have time to do. One of the most impressive achievements of these societies has been the chance they have given thousands of ordinary people to create, develop and participate in their own organisation.

Since British family history societies are run by amateurs, they cannot undertake involved research for their members although they can often unite them with someone willing to check a census entry at the county record office. Usually, they have London contacts who will search in the capital's repositories at economic rates.

For more extensive research the Association of Genealogists and Record Agents (AGRA) (*) will provide a list of professional member agents who have agreed to abide by a detailed code of practice. You can find the names of professional researchers through family history society magazines. Most repositories mentioned in this book will furnish enquirers with a list of local researchers. It is, however, in your interests to be very specific about the work you want doing!

A list of virtually all the existing family history societies and their addresses can be obtained from the Federation of Family History Societies (*). .

UNTRODDEN TERRITORY?

There is a slight chance that someone has already researched or even published some part of your family's history. The probability of linking up with such work naturally increases as you follow your various lines further back into the past.

Any published family history should be mentioned in TR Thomson's *Catalogue of British Family Histories* (3rd ed, 1980). Dr GW Marshall noted pedigrees and family histories included in books he looked at. His final list appeared as *The Genealogist's Guide* (1903, reprinted 1967). This process was continued by JB Whitmore in *A Genealogical Guide* (1953) and GB Barrow in *The Genealogist's Guide* (1977).

All three should be consulted - you would need to visit a large library. Remember, however, that before the 1970s pedigree research was largely the preserve of the well-to-do, and the family histories that they published rarely dealt with the common man.

For other parts of the UK, see Margaret Stuart's *Scottish Family History* (1930); Joan Ferguson's *Scottish Family Histories held in Scottish Public Libraries* (1964); and Brian de Breffny's *Bibliography of Irish Family History and Genealogy* (1974).

The Mormon IGI is primarily an index to parish registers (see p77) but is also an avenue to the 8,000,000 family group records submitted by church members. Entries with all-figure batch numbers (eg 7732623) and with batch numbers prefixed with 'A' refer to such sheets: photocopies can be obtained from the Genealogical Department of the Mormon Church (*) at a small charge. You must supply serial and batch numbers from the IGI. These records need checking - they may contain inaccuracies.

Most family history society magazines have become an economical and accessible forum for the publication of short family histories. The Society of Genealogists (*) holds a card index of all such articles published since 1976, before which only a few societies existed.

Contact family historians working on your surnames through one of the annual directories, advertised by family history societies and by the magazine *Family Tree*. Titles include *National Genealogical Directory* and *Genealogical Research Directory*. Probably the largest, however, is *Family History Knowledge*, with the research interests of 7,300 people included in the 1992/3 edition.

The Family Registry is a microfiche index of millions of surname interests. Updated regularly by the Mormons, it can be consulted freely at their Family History Centres. Similarly accessible is the Mormons' *Ancestral File*, containing on compact disc genealogical research findings on millions of people.

Many hundreds of 'one name' societies have burgeoned over the last decade. Most produce a newsletter, and collect all references to their surname - eg Talbot, Todd. The *Register of One-Name Studies* lists all such surnames and their societies, and is available at £4.30, including UK postage, from the Federation of Family History Societies (*).

KEEPING IN TOUCH

Any serious researcher needs Markwell & Saul (**33**), an encyclopedia of definitions, with references to specialised books. Family history tends to be highly individual, and any researcher's background reading will reflect this. To keep abreast of relevant publications I would advise the following steps:

1) Read one of the nationally circulated magazines. The explosion of interest in family history has brought thousands of publications onto the market. They range from alphabetical lists of (say) Lancashire people in other counties ('strays') to excellent monographs on specific topics - for example merchant seamen's records and First World War sources. All these are reviewed in:

a) *Family Tree Magazine* - available monthly (price £1.65 from bookshops, newsagents and through family history societies). It features sources, family histories, a question and answer page, book reviews, readers' surname interests, and news on changes in the facilities offered by national and county repositories.

b) *Family History News and Digest* - available half yearly (£4.00 including UK postage for two issues) from the FFHS (*) or through individual societies. As well as news content, it provides information on specialist indexes (eg of coastguards, Lancashire miners, soldiers and 16th Century sailors compiled by individuals or groups from all available sources). Perhaps most usefully, it has summaries of the activities of each of the county societies, together with digests of all the articles that have appeared in their magazines. The back pages carry contact addresses of the 171 societies which constitute the Federation.

2) Use libraries and record offices on research outings to spend a little time reading secondary sources - local histories of the towns, villages, and occupations of your ancestors. In one local history published in 1860, I found a detailed description of the Smethwick glass manufactory in which my ROBSON ancestors worked. My wife's Yorkshire coast fishing families have led us into a lifelong interest in fishing vessels and techniques - and it was only a study of these, in turn, which helped us to uncover and understand these families' migration from East Anglia to Filey and Scarborough in the late 18th and early 19th Centuries.

Hey (**32**) and Rogers & Smith (**34**) are excellent on the strong interplay between family and local history, each urging us to look at community as well as family .

SOME HOMILIES

1) **Collect all family information** - proceed up the lines that interest you most, but never write the others off. Gain experience, and come back to problems.

2) **Be honest** - claim nothing you cannot prove.

3) **Keep neat notes** - work for posterity, as well as for your own curiosity.

4) Keep a record of your working - like the solution to a maths problem, a family tree is worthless without the steps that led to its compilation. This is especially important where an ancestor has only been slotted in after some taxing mental effort - don't simply keep the proof in your head.

5) Go back to sources - they always mean more to you each time you use them.

6) Never be afraid to **contact people.** If I hadn't written to my Great Aunt Polly in New Zealand, I would never have learned of the existence of my father's cousin Frank. He told me about the photograph of the American Civil War soldier which hung on the wall in his childhood. Through this I discovered that a wad of documents survived at the National Archives, Washington DC, on my great great grandfather, Edward GATENBY, who left a wife and four daughters in Manchester to go to the USA. There, he married bigamously (twice), enlisted in a Union artillery unit, and suffered a horrible gunshot wound at the Battle of Shiloh in 1862 which resulted in broken leg bones overlapping and shortening the limb by four inches. (Incidentally, emigrant branches of the family are more likely to hoard 'old country' ancestral photographs than the stay-at-homes.)

If you are interested in a surname in an area, try writing to all bearers of that name living there now. I have used the telephone directory on several occasions to send copies of my relevant pedigree to the 20 or so people with that surname - with numbers as small as this, the process always produces relatives. On one occasion, I was sent a copy of a 1935 letter which confirmed that Edward GATENBY had gone to the USA; and on another I discovered details of a diary which had references to my ancestors as early as the 1790s.

A friend of mine visited a 1929 address that he found in the national index to probate grants. The present occupants knew nothing, but the neighbours had known the family 40 years before and sent him to the living representatives - three elderly sisters who gave him a photograph of his great great grandfather.

7) Write it up - once on paper, it has a real chance of surviving. Help your descendants - future generations will find genealogy difficult. Everybody is more geographically mobile than their grandparents; censuses no longer record birthplace; and family sinews which keep us familiar with our ancestors and their haunts are being sliced - 40% of marriages are expected to end in divorce, and 750,000 children never see their fathers, or, one assumes, their paternal grandparents. Illegitimacy rates have risen from around 4% in 1900 to 30% in 1990 (although it is gratifying that 73% of such babies are registered jointly by cohabiting parents). As a result of such social changes, researchers in the next millenium may well have to accept more blanks on their pedigrees than we do. But it is the medical advances of the 1980s which may graft entirely false branches onto some future trees, since the birth certificate of a child born through a surrogacy arrangement carries no hint that its biological parentage is concealed. Yet science also offers an almost biologically cast-iron civil register - should we family historians be lobbying for compulsory DNA fingerprinting?

FURTHER READING

32 David Hey, *Family History and Local History* (Longman,1987)

33 FC Markwell & P Saul, *The Family Historian's Enquire Within* (FFHS,1994)

34 Colin Rogers & John Smith, *Local Family History in England* (Manchester University Press, 1991)

ADDRESSES CITED (*) IN THE TEXT

Although those organisations which are open to the public have normal office hours, it is wise to check the current arrangements in advance of calling.

Association of Genealogists and Record Agents (AGRA), Secretary, 29 Badgers Close, Horsham, West Sussex RH12 5RU

British Newspaper Library, Colindale Ave, London NW9 5HE (tel:071 323 7357)

Commonwealth War Graves Commission, 2 Marlow Rd, Maidenhead, Berkshire SL6 7DX

The Divorce Registry, Somerset House, Strand, London WC2R 1LP (tel:071 936 7016)

Federation of Family History Societies, Benson Room, Birmingham and Midland Institute, Margaret St, Birmingham B3 3BS

General Register Office, St Catherine's House, 10 Kingsway, London WC2B 6JP

General Register Office, Postal Applications Section, Smedley Hydro, Trafalgar Rd, Southport, Merseyside PR8 2HH (tel:051 471 4800)

Land Registry, 32 Lincoln's Inn Fields, London WC2A 3PH (tel:071 917 8888)

Ministry of Defence, Bourne Ave, Hayes, Middlesex UB3 1RF

Mormon Church - Family History Department, 50 East North Temple St, Salt Lake City, Utah 84150, USA

Principal Registry of the Family Division, Correspondence Section, Record Keeper's Department, Somerset House, Strand, London WC2R 1LP (tel:071 936 7454)

Probate Sub-Registry, Duncombe Place, York YO1 2EA

Public Record Office, Chancery Lane, London WC2A 1LR (tel:081 876 3444) - **to be closed at the end of 1996 and all holdings transferred to Kew**

Public Record Office, Ruskin Ave, Kew, Richmond, Surrey, TW9 4DU (tel:081 876 3444)

The Society of Genealogists, 14 Charterhouse Buildings, Goswell Rd, London EC1M 7BA (tel:071 251 8799)

CHANNEL ISLANDS

Guernsey

The Registrar, Ecclesiastical Court, Constables' Office, St Peter Port, Guernsey

The Registrar General of Births, Marriages and Deaths, Greffe, Royal Court House, St Peter Port, Guernsey (tel:0481 725277)

Jersey

Judicial Greffier, 16 Hill St, St Helier, Jersey

Societe Jersiaise, The Museum, Pier Rd, St Helier, Jersey

The Superintendent Registrar, States' Offices, Royal Square, St Helier, Jersey (tel:0534 502335)

ISLE OF MAN

General Registry, Finch Rd, Douglas, Isle of Man IM1 2SB (tel:0624 685242)

Manx Museum and National Trust, Library and Art Gallery, Kingswood Grove, Douglas, Isle of Man (tel: 0624 675522)

EIRE

General Register Office, Joyce House, 8-11 Lombard St East, Dublin 2 (tel:0001 (from UK) 671 1000)

National Archives of Ireland, Bishop Street, Dublin 8 (tel:0001 (from UK) 478 3711)

Registry of Deeds, Henrietta St, Dublin 7 (tel:0001 (from UK) 873 3300)

NORTHERN IRELAND

General Register Office, Oxford House, 49-55 Chichester St, Belfast BT1 4HL (tel:0232 526942)

Public Record Office of Northern Ireland, 66 Balmoral Ave, Belfast BT9 6NY (tel:0232 661621)

Ulster Historical Foundation, 12 College Square East, Belfast BT1 6DD (tel:0232 332288)

SCOTLAND

Association of Scottish Genealogists and Record Agents, 51/3 Mortonhall Rd, Edinburgh EH9 2HN (professional research)

Court of Session, 1 Parliament Square, Edinburgh (tel:031 225 2595)

General Register Office for Scotland, New Register House, Princes St, Edinburgh EH1 3YT (tel:031 314 4427)

e Scottish Record Office, HM General Register House, Edinburgh EH1 3YY (tel:031 556 35)

ots Ancestry Research Society, 29B Albany St, Edinburgh EH1 3QN (tel:031 556 4220) ofessional research)

NATIONAL REPOSITORIES IN LONDON

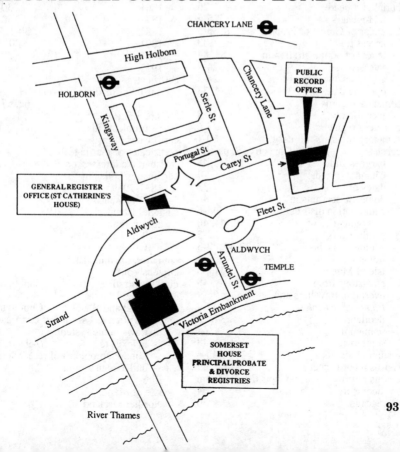

INDEX